in
Amsterdam
– a new look

REG BUTLER

In Association with

THOMSON HOLIDAYS

SETTLE PRESS

While every reasonable care has been taken by the author and publisher in presenting the information in this book, no responsibility can be taken by them or by Thomson Holidays for any inaccuracies. Information and prices were correct at time of printing.

Text © 1989 Reg Butler
Seventh Edition 1997

All rights reserved. No part of this publication may be reproduced or transmitted in any form or by any means without permission.
First published by Settle Press
10 Boyne Terrace Mews
London W11 3LR

ISBN (Paperback) 1 872876 50 1

Printed by Villiers Publications
19 Sylvan Avenue
London N3 2LE
Map film pp 12-13 supplied by Beetwee den Haag

Foreword

As Britain's leading short breaks specialist, we clearly recognise the need for detailed information and guidance for you, the would-be traveller. Yet a Citybreak is about more than museum opening times and table d'hôte tariffs. It's a quite sudden and easy submersion in the continental lifestyle – albeit for only a few days.

We are therefore very pleased to work with Reg Butler and Settle Press on the City Breaks series. Reg Butler has provided for us a very readable book packed not only with important practical information but with colourful observations in a personal style that captures the very essence of your City Break city.

As well as City Breaks in Amsterdam, you will find on the bookshelves City Breaks in Vienna, Salzburg, Prague, Paris, Rome, Florence, Venice, Madrid, Barcelona, Granada, Seville, Bruges, Brussels, Dublin and New York. Of course Thomson operate to many other cities in Europe and the Americas from departure points across the UK.

We're sure you'll find this book invaluable in planning your short break in Amsterdam.

In this revised edition, all opening times, prices, phone numbers and restaurant recommendations have been checked by Thomson's resident staff in Amsterdam. Working there year-round, they have the huge advantage of being able to monitor changes as they happen. Inevitably, more changes will occur between the date of printing and when the reader travels. But this guide-book should still be the most up-to-date on the market!

THOMSON CITYBREAKS

Contents

		Page
1.	**INTRODUCTION**	
	1.1 Go Dutch in Amsterdam	7
	1.2 Which season?	9
2.	**ARRIVAL IN AMSTERDAM**	
	2.1 Schiphol Airport	11
	2.2 Hotel check-in	16
3.	**ORIENTATION**	
	3.1 The city layout	17
	3.2 The principal squares	17
	3.3 Main streets and waterways	18
	3.4 Public transport	19
4.	**DON'T MISS THE HIGHLIGHTS**	
	4.1 The big ten	24
	4.2 Rijksmuseum	25
	4.3 Van Gogh Museum	26
	4.4 Interlude by canal boat	27
5.	**AMSTERDAM ON FOOT**	
	5.1 The central area	29
	5.2 A canal walk	33
	5.3 The Jordaan	35
6.	**WORTH A VISIT**	
	6.1 Buildings and Monuments	37
	6.2 Museums and Galleries	39
7.	**HOLLAND ON DAY TRIPS**	
	7.1 Using Amsterdam as base	44
	7.2 Polders, cheese and windmills	46
	7.3 Bulbs and cut flowers	49
	7.4 Cities to explore	50
8.	**ARCHITECTURAL DELIGHT**	
	8.1 The making of Amsterdam	53
	8.2 Looking at buildings	55

		Page
9.	**GO SHOPPING**	
	9.1 Browsing around the shops	57
	9.2 The main shopping areas	58
	9.3 Department stores	59
	9.4 Street markets	60
	9.5 Buying the Dutch specialities	61
10.	**EATING OUT**	
	10.1 Dutch cuisine	65
	10.2 Restaurant guide	68
	10.3 Typical Dutch snacks	73
	10.4 Guide to the menu	74
11.	**NIGHTLIFE**	
	11.1 See Amsterdam lit up	79
	11.2 The music scene	81
	11.3 Quenching your thirst	81
12.	**TRAVEL TIPS**	
	12.1 Clued-up for Amsterdam	85
	12.2 Taking the children	87
	12.3 Recommended reading	88
	12.4 Learn some Dutch	88
13.	**SUNDAY IN AMSTERDAM**	
	13.1 The joy of peaceful traffic	90
	13.2 Sunday excursions	91
14.	**AT YOUR SERVICE**	
	14.1 Money and banking	92
	14.2 Post Office and Telephone	94
	14.3 Medical	96
	14.4 More information	96

Maps

Amsterdam	12-13
Amsterdam Central Area	14-15
North & South Holland	45

Chapter One
Introduction

1.1 Go Dutch in Amsterdam

For a quick Continental weekend or city break holiday, Amsterdam comes next in popularity after Paris. There is great sightseeing, sparkling nightlife, hundreds of friendly bars and good restaurants. You can feast your eyes on world-famous paintings, and listen to every grade of music from symphonic and ballet, to jazz or folk.

Amsterdam's reputation as a lively short-break destination began in the swinging 'sixties. The accent has changed. Hippies have turned yuppie, but the entertainment and social scene remains lively and tolerant. Some visitors go mainly for the culture, and save their strength for next day's sightseeing around Amsterdam's 42 museums, 141 art galleries, 52 theatres and concert halls.

Other pleasure-seekers prefer another liberal chaser of *jenever* (Dutch gin) with their beer, in the city's 1400 cafés and bars; or they sample the 36 discos that are still spinning long past midnight. Taking a more sober view, Amsterdam has counted 575 coffeeshops, mostly brewing it strong – though the Dutch claim to have invented coffee with milk.

On the architectural front, Amsterdam ranks high among the world's most beautiful cities. In the 16th and 17th centuries, the Dutch capital was the richest trading city in Europe. During that golden age of Amsterdam's prosperity, wealthy merchants built splendid red-brick houses alongside a town-planned ring of canals. Today, those mellowed buildings are fiercely preserved, though modernised within. But,

INTRODUCTION

despite all the antiquity and Old World charm, Amsterdam is a thriving and efficient 20th-century city.

Shutterbugs have a hundred picture possibilities: mellow brick mansions, reflections, bridges and houseboats, all gracefully framed by elm trees. The Dutch use potted plants instead of curtains, and most windows look like crowded greenhouses. On summer evenings, and several times weekly during winter, all the main canal buildings are beautifully illuminated.

Amsterdam claims 160 canals with 70 miles of waterway and over a thousand bridges. Major canals are lined with houseboats – 2400 altogether, many of them furnished in luxury style, complete with a normal Dutch window display of a mini-forest of cacti and potted blooms.

After a sightseeing cruise aboard one of Amsterdam's 70 glass-topped canal boats, you can wander for hours, exploring on your own – following a canal bank past the Floating Flowermarket, crossing a bridge, drifting at random down a narrow side-alley to yet another canal. The city is very compact, with all its historical, cultural and entertainment attractions handily close to each other.

Strolling around, you can enjoy Holland in miniature, with unforgettable small memories at every corner. In an open-air market, old men with Rembrandt faces gossip beside a fish stall, and eat raw herring with chopped onion. The smell of fish mingles with the neighbouring aroma of roasted nuts, and the scent from a profusion of cut flowers. Bakery stalls sell a variety of warm, fresh bread, home-made biscuits and waffles.

Several times daily you'll hear the jaunty music of a traditional Dutch organ – very large, and richly decorated. Keep your ears alert for the melodic chimes of the carillon on the Mint Tower on Muntplein. For classic music, remember that Amsterdam is home town of the world-famed Concertgebouw symphony orchestra. Performances are given mainly between mid-September and March; and also during the annual Holland Festival of music, dance and ballet in June. Year-round,

INTRODUCTION

dozens of bars and clubs feature live Jazz, Soul, New Wave, Latin, African and folk-pop groups at moderate entrance fees or drink prices.

On the culture-vulture circuit, Holland is an art-lovers' Mecca. Amsterdam's Rijksmuseum is supreme in Dutch School, with entire galleries of Rembrandt, Vermeer, Jan Steen and Pieter de Hooch. Crowds are always thickest around *The Night Watch*.

For more Rembrandt, go to Jodenbreestraat where etchings and drawings are displayed in the house where the artist lived almost 20 years until hard times and a lavish lifestyle made him bankrupt. The Municipal Museum (behind the Rijksmuseum) is devoted to modern art. The Van Gogh Museum on the same square houses 200 of the artist's paintings.

1.2 Which season?

Amsterdam is always in season. Springtime is highly popular, especially around the Easter holiday, when Amsterdam can be combined with bulbfield tours. Throughout summer there is a full programme of special events, and the city is well packed with visitors during the July-August peak. All through summer is a good time for enjoying canalside walks, and relaxing in the outdoor cafés and terraces.

With the coming of autumn, museums are less crowded, so that you can admire the collections at leisure.

During winter, the cultural season is at its most vigorous, with numerous concerts and performances in attractive theatres every night. With luck and low-enough temperature, you can even go ice-skating on the canals, just like in a Bruegel painting.

It's a shame to visit Amsterdam without seeing something of the countryside which inspired the Dutch School landscape artists. Holland is usually pictured as a land of glowing tulip fields, with windmills beside every canal, and countryfolk dressed in clogs and national costume. That's about

INTRODUCTION

as 'true' as promoting Britain as a land of thatched cottages, guard-changing ceremonies and quaint olde-worlde customs. However, it's the traditional scene that most visitors prefer.

Most of tourist Holland is on Amsterdam's doorstep: bulb-fields in the Spring; beaches and sand-dunes in summer; Haarlem, blue-pottery Delft or The Hague any time. Make the Dutch capital your base, and you can reach most places by electric train or tour coach within an hour. The travel itself is a pleasure, through flat countryside packed with interest. With distances so small, fares will not sink the holiday budget.

If you prefer to sit back on a guided coach tour, there are half-day excursions to the eel-fishing villages of Marken and Volendam (where the locals actually do wear traditional costume, including clogs); to the Friday cheese market at Alkmaar during summer season; or to The Hague and Delft. If you're desperate for windmill pictures, go to Zaanse Schans where old-tyme Holland has been reconstructed just outside Amsterdam, en route to the Edam-cheese belt.

According to a local saying 'God made the world, but Dutchmen made Holland'.

Almost one-half of Holland lies below sea level. The engineering is worth studying - the layout of canals and dykes, with drainage-ditches that separate the polder fields as effectively as hedges. The long process of reclamation can be seen on the Volendam excursion to Waterland, a short distance north of Amsterdam. The former Zuyder Zee is now a diminishing lake called IJsselmeer, separated from the North Sea by an 18-mile dyke.

One point stands out: an Amsterdam break is hassle-free. It seems like every Dutchman can double-switch into excellent English. Non-linguistic Brits needn't waste time over phrase-books, but can just concentrate on enjoying the enormous variety that Amsterdam can offer. Split your time between museums, shopping, excursions, entertainment, sightseeing, drinking in brown bars or eating in cosy restaurants. Your only regret will be that your city break isn't longer.

Chapter Two
Arrival in Amsterdam

2.1 Schiphol Airport

Air travellers to Amsterdam are offered nationwide departure options when they fly from UK. Bulk of the traffic is shared between British Airways, and KLM Royal Dutch Airlines and its regional subsidiary KLM Cityhopper.

KLM operates frequent daily services from Manchester and Heathrow Terminal 4, using Boeing 737's or Airbus A310. Cityhopper uses smaller commuter aircraft such as the Saab 340B and Fokker 50 from a number of regional airports.

With the addition of flights by partner carriers, such as Air UK in which KLM has a 15% stake, and Transavia (80% owned by KLM) there are 25 airports in UK and Ireland with direct links to Schiphol. A great time-saving convenience for those wanting a short break in Amsterdam!

Likewise, Schiphol has extremely convenient connections into Amsterdam's city centre. If no tour-operator transfer is included, then the easiest route into Amsterdam is by train to Central Station – costing 6.00 guilders for the 20-minute journey, with several trains an hour. You never wait more than 15 minutes. It's worth remembering this route for the return journey – far cheaper than taxi, costing around 65 guilders. Incidentally, luggage trolleys can be used on escalators.

As alternative to air travel, you can take the fast track by Eurostar from London or Ashford to Brussels, with onward connection to Amsterdam for an overall journey time of 6 hours 45 minutes.

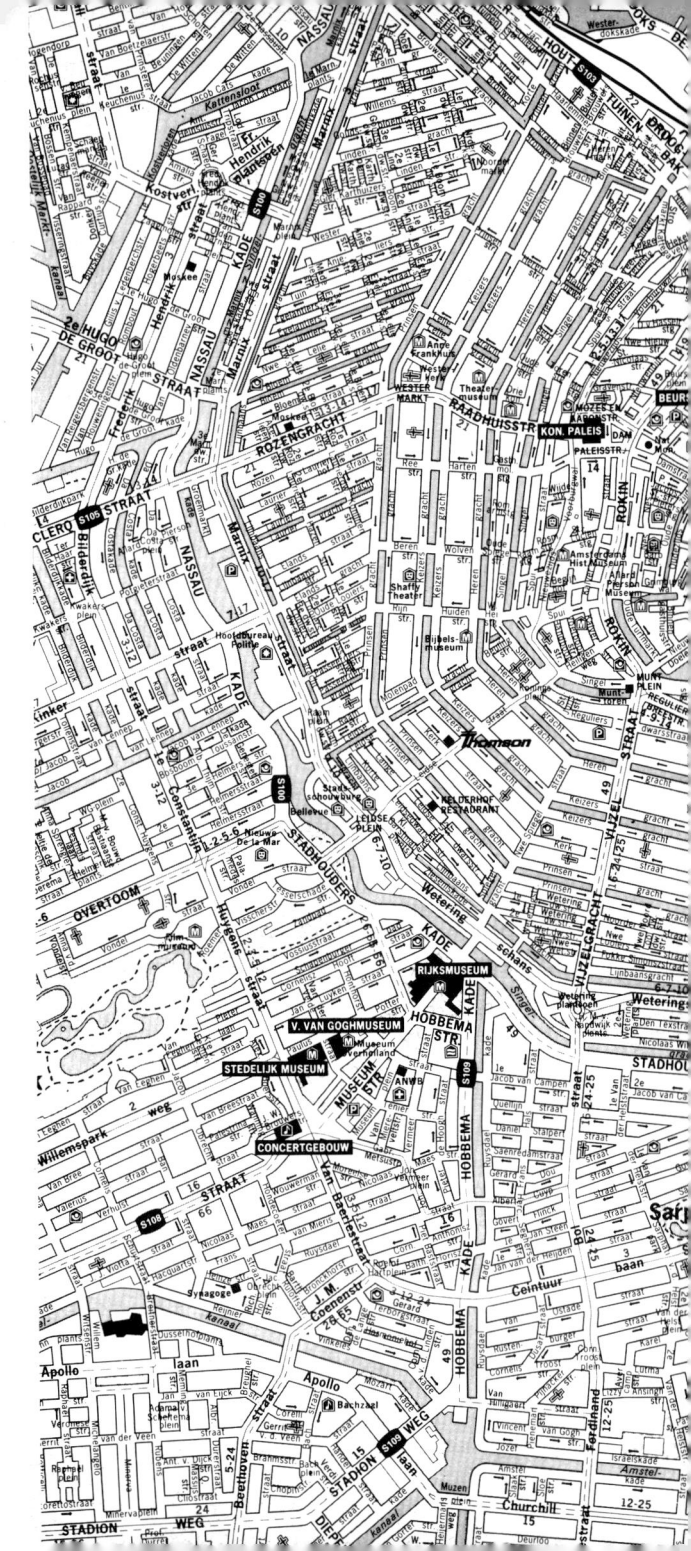

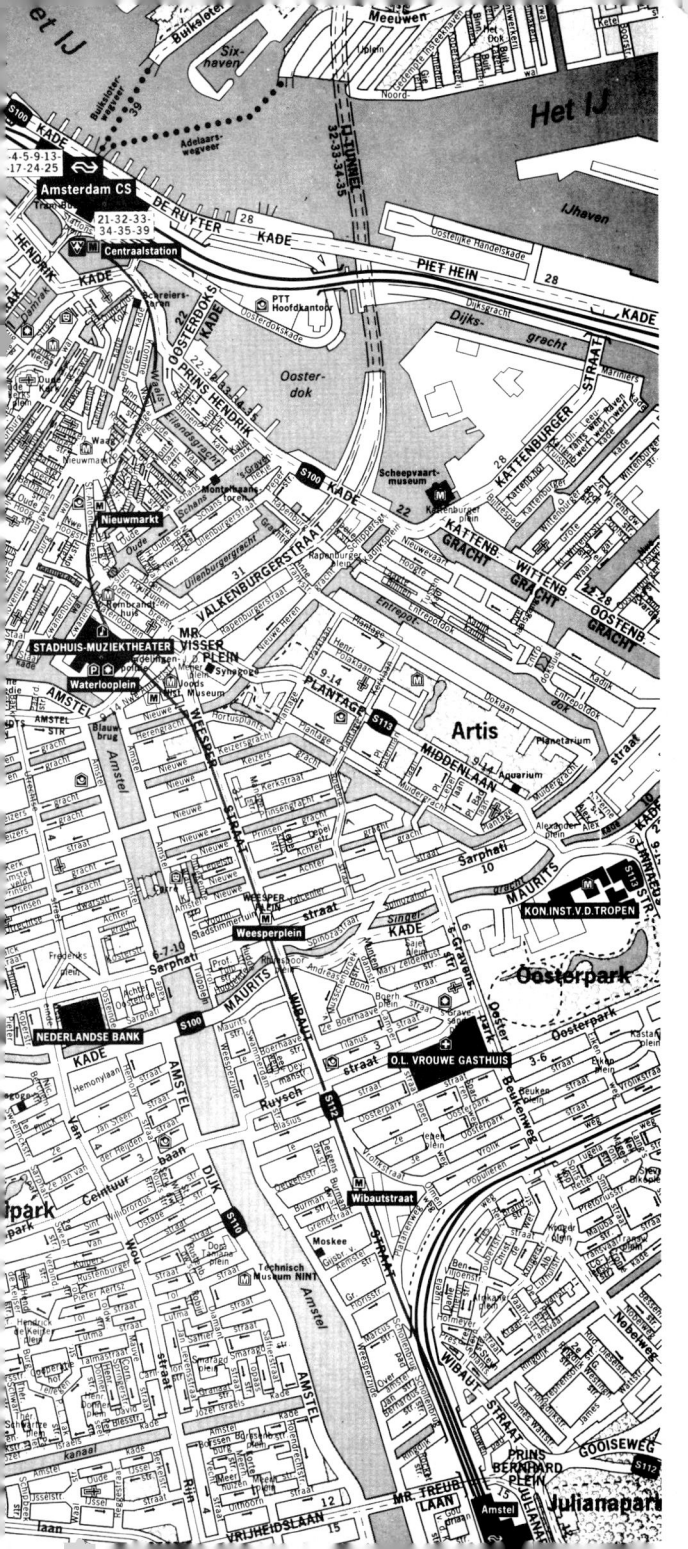

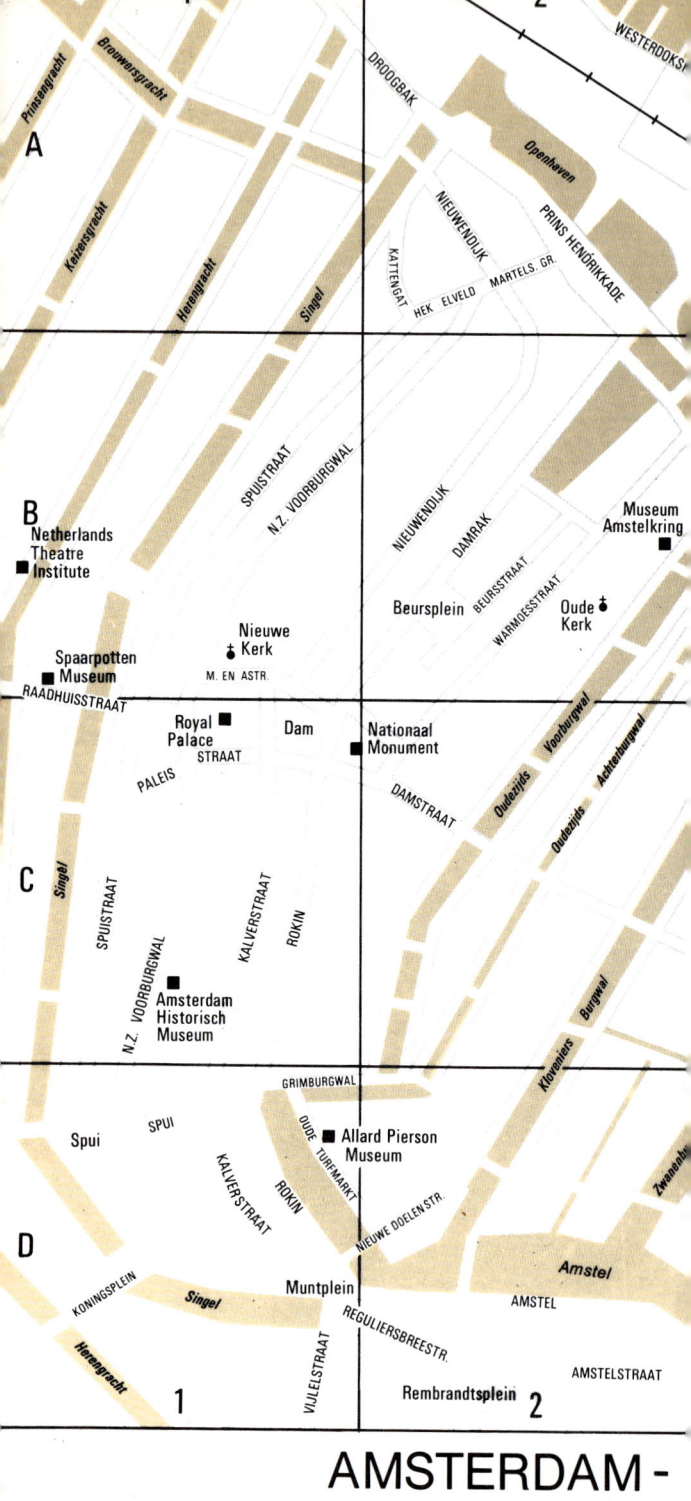

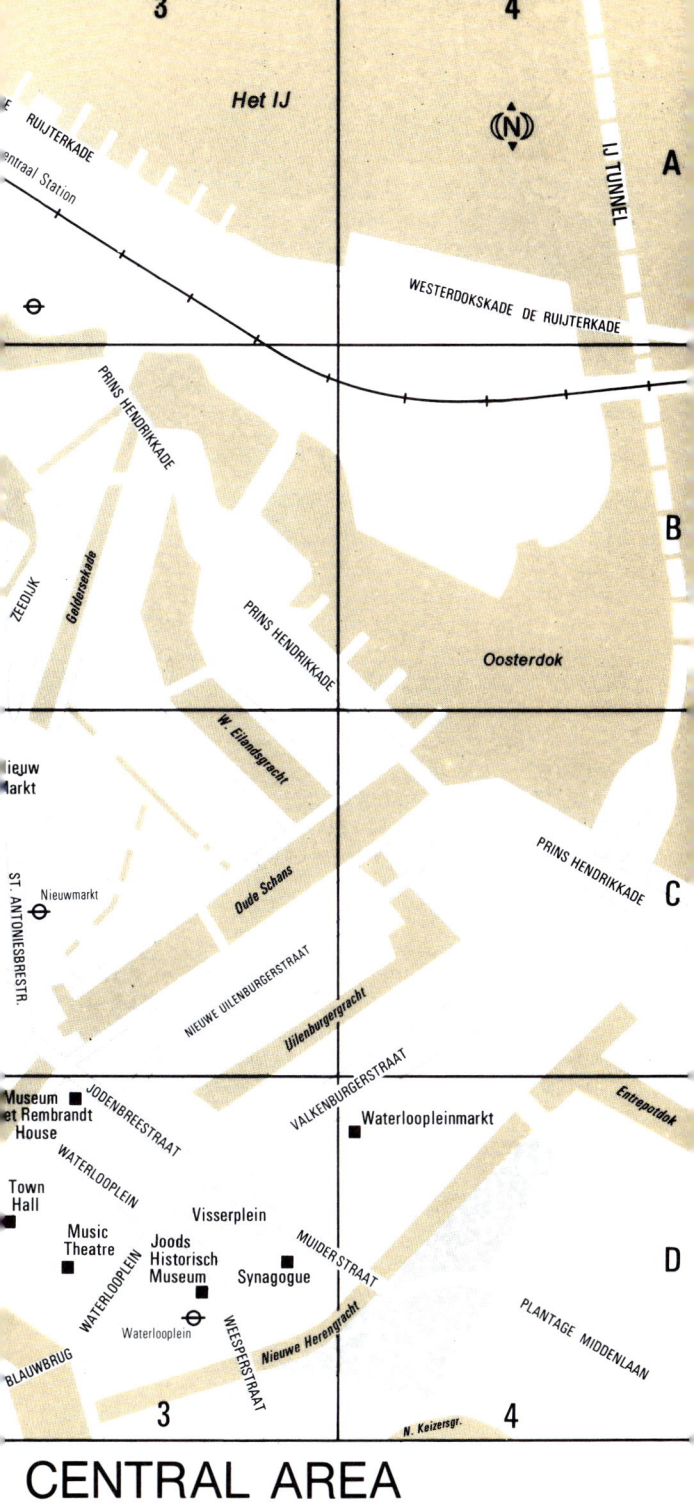

ARRIVAL

2.2 *Hotel check-in*

Checking-in and out time in hotels is generally midday, but confirm with reception. If you arrive early your room may not be ready. But check in and leave your cases in the hotel.

On departure day remember to vacate your room by midday. Hotel management will be pleased to look after your luggage at reception.

Most hotels of two stars upwards have TV's, and you can normally pick up BBC 1 and 2, besides the local stations and satellite channels like CNN.

Safety Deposit Boxes

Most hotels have either a safe or safety deposit boxes for your valuables. Use this service from the moment you arrive at your hotel, for safe keeping of cash, traveller's cheques, passports and travel documents. There's no reason to wander around Amsterdam with passport and flight tickets, which cause enormous inconvenience if lost.

Lighting

Hotel corridors sometimes have a time switch for the lights, to allow enough time to unlock your door. Look for a small orange light and press the button.

Getting in late

Some hotels have a night porter, so if you arrive back late just ring the bell. Others give you two keys which you keep at all times – one for your room and the other for the front door.

Stairs

As Amsterdam's houses are tall and narrow, the stairs in many of the hotels are very steep, and some hotels in lower categories do not have a lift.

Voltage

220 volts and standard continental-type 2-pin plugs.

Chapter Three
Orientation

3.1 The city layout

In Dutch, Dam means 'dyke'. Dam Square is the central square of Amsterdam, the Piccadilly Circus which is the city's transport focal point. As a large square with the rarely-used Royal Palace as the principal building, Dam doubles as an international youth rendezvous with buskers and international gossip.

To get yourself better oriented, here's a checklist of Amsterdam locations. Fix them on the map, and you'll soon know your way around. Particularly note Amsterdam's basic fan-shaped plan for the inner city – radiating from Central Station, with the girdles of canal belts setting a concentric pattern.

3.2 The principal squares

Stationsplein – The square in front of Central Station, the main traffic terminal for trains, Metro, buses and trams. All Amsterdam fans out from this point.

Leidseplein, **Rembrandtsplein** and **Thorbeckeplein** – the three main centres of tourist bars, restaurants and entertainment. (See chapter 11).

Museumplein – location for the big three art galleries: Rijksmuseum, Van Gogh Museum and Stedelijk Museum. On the outside wedge of the square is the 100-years-old Concertgebouw – world-famed for its resident symphony orchestra.

ORIENTATION

Muntplein – a major traffic intersection, close to Rembrandtsplein, with Mint Tower, Floating Flower Market and at the meeting-point of River Amstel with Singel and the main canals of the Old Side of central Amsterdam.

Waterlooplein – The original area of Jewish settlement, Waterlooplein is now occupied by the new City Hall. The Muziek Theater – the ultra-modern Opera House – forms part of the complex. The Rembrandt House is one block away, on Jodenbreestraat, number 6. Waterlooplein's famous Flea Market is situated in front of the new Opera House. Also near by is the Jewish Historical Museum on **J.D. Meijerplein**.

3.3 Main streets and waterways

Het IJ – the harbour and dock area.

Damrak – linking Stationsplein and Dam Square.

Kalverstraat – one of the main shopping streets, from Dam Square to Muntplein, giving access to Amsterdam Historical Museum, the Begijnhof and Madame Tussaud's.

Rokin – from Dam Square, is the continuation of Damrak, leading to Muntplein; a good shopping street, parallel to Kalverstraat.

Leidsestraat – One of Amsterdam's most popular shopping zones. Leidsestraat is banned to cars, but pedestrians must still stay alert for trams and bicycles.

Singel – Running in a semi-circle from Het IJ to the Amstel River, Singel was formerly the moat which protected the original city.

Herengracht, Keizersgracht & Prinsengracht – the triple girdle of concentric canals, a city-planned development in 17th century.

ORIENTATION

Leidsegracht & Reguliersgracht – two of the principal canals that link the 'big three' canals. The fan-shaped pattern enclosed by these canals makes the most rewarding area for sightseeing of 'golden age' Amsterdam.

Singelgracht – the outermost big canal, marking the limits of the main 17th-century city, and the beginnings of the 19th-century developments. Don't confuse it with Singel! The outer bank comprises a useful orientation road for motorists – city-route number S 100, running like a ring road around the old centre, changing its name from Mauritskade to **Stadhouderskade** and thence to Nassaukade. The prime tourist section is from Leidseplein across to Vondelpark entrance and to the Rijksmuseum.

Oudezijds Voorburgwal & Achterburgwal – parallel canals through the heart of Old Amsterdam, formerly moats that protected the original city walls. This is the Red Light district.

Vondelpark – Laid out in the 19th century, all part of the development from Leidseplein to the Rijksmuseum, Vondelpark is a lively summertime rendezvous both for Amsterdammers and for tourists. Sunday afternoon is specially crowded, relaxed and tolerant. Informal entertainment is a big attraction: from a wide variety of buskers, to theatre, music and poetry readings.

Many of the hippies who camped here during the love-ins and the demonstrations of the 60's and 70's have now become very designer orientated, selling handmade jewelry and ornaments.

3.4 Public transport

Most Amsterdam hotels are located within an easy walk of tightly-bunched main sights. Central Amsterdam is very compact. If you concentrate on one sector each day, there's little need to make great use of public transport.

To reach your day's starting-point, take a tram or bus. After midnight, the trams stop running; but

ORIENTATION

there are special night buses. Otherwise, if you're not within convenient walking distance of your destination, take a taxi. Because of parking problems, car hire is useless except for out-of-town trips.

Amsterdam is very well served by public transport. Most visitors make good use of the 16 tram routes, but buses and a limited Metro system provide good connections. The brightly coloured trams are fun to use.

Each tram shelter has a map showing the network of tram lines, and also a list of subsequent stops to be made. It's a good check that you are travelling in the right direction!

As mentioned earlier, the network radiates from Stationsplein – the square in front of Central Station. Call there at the GVB information office, or at the ticket kiosk on Leidseplein, to buy either a Day Card or a 15-strip ticket – see details below.

Ask for a route map, with an English-language explanation. It's worth taking a few minutes to learn the system.

Day Cards

The easiest way of riding trams, buses and the Metro system is to buy a Day Card costing 12.00 Dfl from a bus or tram driver.

Cards should be stamped the first time of use, to validate them. Stamping machines are yellow, and are located at rear and front inside the trams.

Strip Tickets

These can be bought from the bus or tram driver in multiples of 2, 3 and 10 at a cost of Dfl 3.00, 4.50 and 11.00 respectively. The driver will stamp the first ticket for you, valid for transfers to other vehicles within one hour.

Thereafter you must stamp two strips for travel within the Central zone. At your first attempt, ask a fellow traveller to demonstrate how it's done.

An even better deal is the 15-strip ticket costing Dfl 11.00, available from the GVB counters opposite Central Station and at Leidseplein, and in post offices. Incidentally, these strip tickets are also valid for tram or bus transport anywhere in the

ORIENTATION

country, depending how many 'zones' you traverse. More than one person can utilise the ticket – just date-stamp the appropriate number of strips.

Occasionally ticket inspectors board the vehicle. Failure to produce a valid ticket entails a fine of Dfl 60.00.

Tram doors open automatically by pressing the 'deur open' button. The bottom step also controls the closing of the door – while you are standing on it, the door is locked in the open position. So keep your foot on it, when helping someone step in or out.

Board buses by the front door, and show the driver your ticket.

Canal Bus

Another transport alternative is to buy a Canal Bus day ticket costing Dfl 19.75. It gives you unlimited rides along different circuits between Central Station (starting from across the canal, opposite the Amsterdam Tourist Office) and the Rijksmuseum.

With three stops along each route, you can hop on and off all day, taking photographs from every angle.

Taxis

A minimum charge of Dfl 5.00 will appear on the meter irrespective of whether you call a taxi or pick one up at a rank. Thereafter the rate is calculated according to the time of day and inner/outer limits.

The meter shows the rate at which the fare is being calculated according to zone. For example, Tariff 1 is used for within the city limits; Tariff 2 is used outside the limits, such as when travelling to the airport.

Cruising taxis do exist, though it is often easier to go to a taxi stand. No additional charges are made for luggage. A small tip is customary.

It is always advisable to ask the driver the approximate cost of your journey.

As a guide, you can expect to pay around Dfl 20.00 per journey within Amsterdam, and roughly Dfl 65.00 between Schiphol Airport and central Amsterdam.

ORIENTATION

Bicycle hire

A word of warning: riding bicycles around the centre can be dangerous, unless you are accustomed to cycling in heavy continental traffic.

However, cycles are excellent for getting out of Amsterdam into the surrounding countryside. Follow one of the many bike paths, for which maps are available from the VVV (Amsterdam Tourist Office.

A convenient location for bike hire is:

Koenders Rent-a-Bike, Central Station, East Side. Tel: 624 8391. Open daily 8-22 hrs. Rental costs Dfl 8.00 per day; Dfl 200.00 deposit. Passport is required, for identity.

NB: Should the bike be stolen or damaged in any way, you must pay the full amount, which is taken from the deposit.

Out-of-town cycling

Holland has been geared up for cycling ever since the invention of the velocipede. With 80% of the population owning a bicycle, the cycling lobby is all-powerful.

Backed by that huge voting power, there has been development of over 6000 miles of special cycling lanes and paths, where motorised vehicles are taboo.

All these cycling lanes are clearly signposted. At every crossing-point there's a white concrete 'mushroom' signpost close to the ground, giving directions, distances and - even more helpful - a reference number which enables you to pinpoint your position anywhere in Holland.

Local tourist maps colour-code three grades of cycle track: surfaced, two metres wide, with or without permission for motorised bikes; and the rest (unsurfaced, or less than two metres wide).

In a casual way, as you ride along the cycle paths, you can start chatting with Dutch riders who want to practise their English, or who just want to be friendly.

Many of the Dutch riders are middle-aged to elderly, just keeping in trim for prolonged enjoyment of their pensions.

ORIENTATION

Canal trips

A 200-yard stroll from Dam – either along Rokin, or to the end of Damrak – and you reach the landing-stage for Amsterdam's best sightseeing buy: a one-hour canal tour by glass-covered launch, with loudspeaker commentary in English, French and German. Price is about £4. You can see everything, without wearing out your feet on the cobbles. See more details in Chapter 4.2.

Another alternative: for around £5 you can hire a two-seater 'Canal Bike' – a pedalo – for two hours; or £7.50 for four hours. A deposit of Dfl 50.00 is required.

A variation on transport is to use a Water Taxi, which can take up to eight passengers. It's an ideal means of transport for Amsterdam, where most of the important locations can be reached by water. Passengers are told in advance what the journey will cost. Phone number is 6222181.

Another possibility for 'different' sightseeing, April till October, is to use the special Museum Boat service which plies a route past nine Amsterdam museums at 30-minute intervals.

This step-on, step-off service costs Dfl 22.00 for the all-day ticket. Starting from the pier in front of the Amsterdam Tourist Office (VVV) at Central Station, the main stops are for Anne Frank House, Madame Tussaud, Amsterdam Historical Museum, Rijksmuseum, Rembrandt House, and Maritime Museum.

Chapter Four
Don't miss the highlights

4.1 The big ten

Amsterdam offers so much to see and do, that it's hard for the first-time visitor to decide on the basic essentials during a city break trip. It is therefore best to take an organised city tour to get an overall view, and from this make a short-list of what you wish to see in more detail. Here are the basics:

(1) Amsterdam on foot: follow one of the routings suggested in Chapter Five.
(2) Visit the Rijksmuseum, if only for the 'Night Watch' and other Rembrandts. (See below).
(3) Also visit the Van Gogh Museum (see below); or the modern art Stedelijk Museum on the same square behind Rijksmuseum. (See Chapter Six).
(4) Take a Canal Cruise by day (see below) or by night (see Chapter Eleven).
(5) Visit a diamond factory to see cutting and polishing (Chapter Nine for addresses).
(6) On a more sombre note, dedicate an hour to the Anne Frank House (see Chapter Six).
(7) Absorb the atmosphere, and the beer, of a 'brown bar' (see Chapter Eleven).
(8) According to taste, try to include a symphony concert; or opera or ballet at the Muziek Theatre; or sample the jazz, folk and disco scene around Leidseplein. (See Chapter Eleven).
(9) Have dinner at an Indonesian restaurant and order *rijsttafel*. (See Chapter Ten)
(10) Take a trip into the Dutch countryside – a Bulbfields Tour between late March and mid-May; or, for those who wish to see how Dutch cheese or

HIGHLIGHTS

clogs are made, go either to Volendam and Marken, or to Zaanse Schans and Edam. (Chapter Seven).

4.2 Rijksmuseum

With one million visitors a year, the Rijksmuseum ranks high among the world's greatest art galleries – certainly the richest in Dutch School.

This National Gallery of the Netherlands owes its origin to Napoleon's brother, King Louis Bonaparte, who started the collection in 1808. Its first home was the Royal Palace on Dam Square. Amsterdam City Council added various works including Rembrandt's 'Night Watch'. Later the collection was moved to the Trippenhuis, one of the grandest of Amsterdam's Golden Age houses.

Overflowing, the ever-growing collection was moved to its present purpose-built quarters. Note the Rijksmuseum's external similarity to Central Station, designed by the same architect and opened in the same year, 1885.

Everyone has to see Rembrandt's 'Night Watch'. Last century, somebody made a blunder in titling this painting. In reality it's a daytime portrait group of a company of civil guards emerging into a pool of *sunlight*. The 'Night' label is explained by the accumulated varnish, candle-smoke and grime, which has since been cleaned off.

Everyone halts before this masterpiece and a selection of the 17 other Rembrandts that cover different phases of the artist's life.

It's quite impossible in a single visit to take more than a quick glance at the remaining collections of Vermeer, Pieter de Hoogh, Frans Hals, Jan Steen and their contemporaries. Don't try to gulp the whole lot in one visit, but seriously make time to come back another day.

Besides Dutch School, the Museum also includes a small selection of foreign art, including works by Goya, Tintoretto and Veronese.

The Rijksmuseum includes several other departments of more specialised interest. These are:

Printroom – an extensive collection of graphic art

HIGHLIGHTS

from several different periods. The exhibition is changed every four months.

Dutch History – focusses mainly on Holland's 'golden age' and on trading and maritime links, particularly with China and Japan.

Sculpture and Applied Art – three floors that cover 11th century to early 20th: furniture, silver and glass, masses of Delft pottery. The 18th-century Dolls' Houses are a delight.

Asiatic Art – includes sculpture, pottery and lacquer work from China, Japan, India and South East Asia.

The Rijksmuseum is located at 42 Stadhouderskade – an easy walk from Leidseplein, past Vondelpark. By public transport, take tram 1, 2 or 5. Numbers 2 and 5 stop at the back door, one stop past Leidseplein.

Open Mon-Sat 10-5. Sun 1-5. Entrance Dfl 10.

4.3 Van Gogh Museum

Opened in 1973, the Museum houses the world's largest collection of works by Vincent van Gogh. Recognised today as the most important Dutch artist of the 19th century, van Gogh first worked as an art dealer, then as a schoolteacher in Ramsgate, and became a self-taught painter at age 27.

He suffered periods of madness. During one outburst he cut off part of his ear; then shot himself in 1890, aged 37. He sold only one canvas in his lifetime. At auction in 1987, his painting 'Irises' fetched 49 million dollars. Since then, other paintings have gone even higher!

The canvases are arranged in chronological order, upstairs on the 1st floor, making it easy to distinguish between his different periods, influences and styles.

From 1880-1887 was van Gogh's heavy brown 'Dutch period', when he was living in southern Holland – peasants, moorland scenes and still life. The most dramatic work of this period was 'The Potato Eaters'.

Then 1887-1890 came his 'Paris period' when van Gogh joined his art-dealer brother Theo. In

HIGHLIGHTS

Paris, his technique changed under the influence of the Impressionists and Neo-Impressionists. He stopped using browns and umbers, and began painting in the clear, bright colours for which he is better known. In 1888 he moved to Arles in southern France, and filled his canvases with sunlight – his most creative period, ending in madness and death.

On the 2nd floor are drawings by van Gogh, plus his own collection of Japanese prints which greatly influenced him during his Paris interlude. The pastels and prints are exhibited in subdued lighting, due to the risk of fading.

The 3rd floor is used for a variety of special exhibitions. The ground floor is devoted to works by van Gogh's contemporaries, including Gauguin, Toulouse-Lautrec, Pisarro and Manet – an impressive selection of pictures collected by Vincent van Gogh himself or by his brother Theo.

Van Gogh Museum is located behind the Rijksmuseum at 7 Paulus Potterstraat. Tram 2, 5. Open Mon-Sat 10-17 hrs; Sun and public holidays 13-17 hrs. Entrance 10.00 Dfl.

4.4 Interlude by canal boat

Give your feet a rest, and take a canal-boat trip. If you have already walked around central Amsterdam, you'll have seen several jetties opposite Central Station. Others are on the Damrak, at the point where Rokin meets Spui, and near Leidseplein, opposite Park Hotel on the Stadhouderskade.

Walking through the Old Side and New Side shows mainly the pre-1612 layout, in the years before the 'Golden Century'. A boat trip can show you magnificent Amsterdam from the viewpoint of the sailors and merchants of 300 years ago – from a foot or two above water level. Afloat, you enter a different and more tranquil age.

The boat trips all have loudspeaker commentary by guides or multi-lingual recorded tapes, with English the main language. The routes taken by the different boat-tour companies do vary. But they all cover similar ground, including some that is best avoided on foot around the Zeedijk.

HIGHLIGHTS

They show you the tiny, narrow Oude Zijds Kolk (a continuation of Voorburgwal); some other sectors of the Old Side such as the Oude Schans (the Old Rampart); the broad River Amstel beyond the end of Rokin, and the famous old Magere Brug (Skinny Bridge); sections of the Singel, the canal that once marked the limits of the New Side.

Outwards from Singel are the famous three canal-rings – Herengracht, Keizersgracht and Prinsengracht – linked by Reguliersgracht and Leidsegracht. There are endless route permutations.

By official count, Amsterdam has 1,281 bridges. Eight are wooden drawbridges. Many of the most decorative are in the New South (Nieuw Zuid) suburbs, outside the regular boat-tour circuits. But those you do see are a good sample.

The longer tours end with a view of the main IJ harbour, with its floating docks, passenger quays and modern installations, along with a glimpse of the locks controlling the flow of water through the city's maze of canals. Because the water level is rigidly controlled, boats are built to clear the bridges by inches, without scalping the passengers.

Chapter Five
Amsterdam on foot

5.1 The central area

The best starting point for getting your bearings in the Dutch capital is either from the Dam Square, or from Central Railway Station. A busy main road called Damrak links the two locations – a five-minute walk, unless you stop to stare at shops or sights en route.

Central Station is not just trains. The Station Square is also main terminus for ten of the city's 16 tram lines, and eleven of the 30 bus routes. Wherever you're staying in Amsterdam, it's very easy to reach.

While you're there, drop in to the VVV Tourist Information Bureau, in front of the main entrance, open 9.00 till 23.00 hrs from Easter through September, or until 17.00 the rest of the year. Pick up any brochures, maps or advice you might need.

At the GVB Amsterdam Municipal Transport Office you can also buy day passes or strip tickets for the transport system (see chapter 3). If you're stuck for guilders, the GWK exchange office is open every day including Sundays until 10.45 p.m., and gives a good rate.

Central Station was built 1885 on an artificial island in Amsterdam's vast sheltered harbour, the stretch of water known as Het IJ (pronounced 'Eye').

With Central Station behind you, cross the very busy bridge towards Damrak. Prins Hendrik Kade (Prince Henry Quay) faces you, left and right. Till 1833, Damrak was part of the River Amstel. In earlier times, ships tied up along Prins Hendrik Kade and along Damrak, to unload their cargoes. Today, the shipping is confined to glass-rooved canal boats and water taxis, as another means of sightseeing Amsterdam.

Old and New Sides
Damrak is relatively modern: shops, restaurants, hotels, offices and a Stock Exchange building. But if you look around – and up – you'll see remains of older gables and a row of fine warehouses, half left across a patch of water. The area to your left is called the 'Old Side' (Oude Zijd). That's the direction, later, if you want to go window-shopping through the Red Light zone.

To your right is 'New Side' (Nieuwe Zijd), which was new around 1400. That side is good for browsing through alleyways that lead off from Damrak to the parallel broad street called Nieuwendijk (New Dyke). All that area is pedestrianized with good shopping, bars galore and choice of restaurants.

Just past the left-hand patch of water with its canal-boat jetties is the Beurs – the Amsterdam Stock Exchange. Though no longer used as an Exchange, the Beurs is a reminder that Amsterdam ranks among Europe's leading financial centres. The innovative structure with exposed girders in the main hall aroused great architectural interest when built in 1898. (See details on page 38).

Further up Damrak, on the right just past the C&A department store is Zoutsteeg, where ships used to unload cargoes of salt (zout) – remember that all this busy highway was formerly part of the Amstel River.

Thence you come into Dam Square. The dominating building is the Royal Palace, befitting Amsterdam's status as the capital of Holland, though the government, civil service and official royal residence are based in The Hague.

The Palace was built between 1648 and 1655 as Amsterdam's Town Hall, supported on 13,659 wooden piles to overcome the problem of a soggy sub-soil. The building was requisitioned by Louis

ON FOOT

Bonaparte in 1808, after his elder brother Napoleon made him King of Holland (1806-1810). When he abdicated, most of his furniture remained.

After being half palace and half town hall for over a century, the building was formally sold off by the City of Amsterdam in 1935. Public visiting hours are brief. The Royal Family's visits are even briefer – never in residence, just commuting in for State occasions.

Right of the Palace is the New Church (Nieuwe Kerk), founded in early 15th century, and so named to distinguish it from the Old Church (Oude Kerk). Burnt down several times, the renewed New Church dates mainly from 17th century. When the Town Hall next door was promoted to rank as a Royal Palace, Nieuwe Kerk likewise was upgraded to become Holland's Coronation Church. Today, apart from suchlike State events, Nieuwe Kerk is used mainly for exhibitions and organ recitals.

Round the back of the Palace was the Central Post Office – worth a look, for its whimsical 'Amsterdam School' of Art Nouveau decoration. Dating from 1908. It's now the Magna Plaza Shopping Centre.

Back in Dam Square, an obelisk commemorates the nation's dead of World War 11. Shallow circles of steps around the monument offer sitting-space for tourists, and a semi-captive audience for itinerant musicians.

The continuation of Nieuwendijk south of the Damplein is a narrow street called Kalverstraat. It is full of shops and is a pedestrian precinct, along with the alleys that lead off it. Turn right at number 92 into Sint Luciensteeg (St. Lucy Alley) and you come to the splendid Amsterdam Historical Museum. Save the Museum for a special visit. Otherwise you'll never finish the walk.

A little further down Kalverstraat gives access to the Begijnhof – see details in chapter 6 – possibly the loveliest of the country's *hofjes* (secluded almshouses). A quiet oasis in the heart of the city, the Begijnhof offers a total contrast to the crowded shopping area around the corner. Pause for pictures!

ON FOOT

From the Begijnhof you soon reach the street (formerly a canal) called the Spui, marked by W.H. Smith's on the corner. Turn left, and cross the Rokin, which is the southward continuation of the Damrak. Walk along the Grimburgwaal to start an exploration of the Old Side, which runs northwards back towards Central Station. Two long canals, the Oude Zijds Voorburgwal and the Oude Zijds Achterburgwal, run right through the area. Each was once the moat of a town wall (burgwal). Where the two canals meet Grimburgwal is a popular shutterbug target, the House on the Three Canals (Huis aan de Drie Grachten).

The southern tip of Oude Zijds is occupied mainly by University of Amsterdam buildings. The administration building is a quiet almshouse built in 1754 and reached by a little lane called Oude Manhuispoort (Old-Man's-Home Gate), which is also a daily secondhand book market.

Coming back to Oude Zijds Voorburgwal, part of the former City Hall (Raadhuis) lies on one side of the canal. The building has been beautifully converted into one of the most elegant hotels in Amsterdam. The entrance courtyard still keeps the original atmosphere.

Further up the canal, left side, is Oude Kerk, oldest of the city's churches. If you're there when the tower is open, it's worth a guilder to climb to the top, for a superb gull's-eye view of old Amsterdam.

A little beyond Oude Kerk is the Amstelkring Museum, which preserves a top-floor 'concealed' Catholic church known as Our Dear Lord in the Attic.

All this area comprises Amsterdam's 'famous' red light district which one is advised to avoid after dark.

Old Side is a wonderful tangle of alleys and waterways, and haphazard drifting can be rewarding. There are attractive old bars in Damstraat, leading off Dam Square. The Zuider Kerk (South Church) in Zandstraat has another fine tower like the Oude Kerk, and a fine carillon. The street called Rusland (Russia) is reputed to commemorate Peter the

ON FOOT

Great's stay in Amsterdam when he was learning about shipbuilding. Many street and canal names are picturesque: Rechtboomsloot (Straight Tree Ditch) and Kromboomsloot (Crooked Tree Ditch), for instance.

Finally, a cautionary note: it's best to avoid Zeedijk (Sea Dyke street). It curves from Central Station to the Waag (weighhouse) which started life as a city gate. Originally, the Zeedijk protected the tiny village of Amstel Dam from the sea, when it was just a hamlet in the parish of Oudekerk. In more recent times, Zeedijk is said to have a name for hard-drug dealing, though efforts have been made to clean up the district.

5.2 A canal walk

After seeing the Grachtengordel (the Canal Girdle of the three great town-planned canals) by boat – see Chapter 4 – try exploring the area on foot. Take it very slowly, looking at details of the individual houses. The exact routing hardly matters. To give a clue on mileage, Herengracht is 1.5 miles long; Keizersgracht 1.7 miles; Prinsengracht 2 miles. The concentric canals are about 100 yards apart, linked by frequent streets or canals, so that switching from one to another is easy. If you're seeing Amsterdam over a weekend, try it by bicycle on a quiet Sunday morning when traffic is asleep.

Most of the canals are now edged with a low railing, to hinder careless car-parking in the water. The canals are nine feet deep, with a thick layer of sludge st the bottom, not recommended for a morning dip. Although the canals look stagnant, locks are opened three times a week and a carefully regulated volume of water flushes through.

A good starting-point is the Muntplein area, which is worth looking around, despite being one of Amsterdam's most hectic traffic intersections (on tram routes 4, 9, 14, 16, 24 and 25). You can get shore-based pictures of sightseeing boats on the several canals that meet the Amstel River.

Alongside the Floating Flowermarket on the Singel is the Mint Tower (Munttoren). The lower

ON FOOT

part was originally the city's mint. The decorative upper part was added in 1620 by Hendrik de Keyser, the period's most outstanding architect and the person most closely associated with the town's expansion.

The Mint Tower's carillon clock has for centuries been Amsterdam's official timekeeper. The carillon was cast 300 years ago by the Hemony brothes from Alsace. They were responsible also for the carillons in the Old Church, South Church, West Church and Royal Palace. The secret of how they tuned the bells was lost when they died and only re-discovered in 1959, since when the carillons have all been retuned.

From Muntplein, stroll along Reguliersbreestraat to the pedestrianized Rembrandtsplein, one of Amsterdam's major nightlife centres, with restaurants, bars, theatres, cinemas and other entertainment. Head due south along Thorbeckeplein to reach Reguliersgracht with its string of seven closely-packed bridges across the three prime waterways of the Canals Girdle.

Turn right along the Herengracht's further side. To live on the Herengracht was high status in the 17th and 18th centuries, and it's still the height of ambition for many Amsterdammers today. Anywhere along the Herengracht was a 'good address', but all the best people (anyway, the wealthiest) lived on the 'Golden Bend' where the canal curves between Vijzelstraat and Leidsestraat.

A suitable house for a gentleman was double-width, with double stairways and a servants' entrance between. Look at No. 424, for instance, and No. 370 and its two fine neighbours – the Cromhout houses built in 1662 for branches of the Cromhout family. Many of the buildings today are used as offices, or converted to elegant small hotels. But the urbane exteriors are well preserved.

Specially look at the great variety of decorative gables. Notice the hoists that protrude from virtually every building. And spot the *spionnetjes* – little spies – like car wing mirrors fixed outside upper windows, so that the occupant can discreetly check who's on the doorstep, ringing the bell.

ON FOOT

5.3 The Jordaan

West of the main central district is the Jordaan, one of the city's most charming areas. Formerly working class, it has become middle-class, bohemian and chic – a centre for arts and crafts, boutiques and colourful brown bars.

The area lies roughly between the west banks of the Prinsengracht and the Lijnbaansgracht, and stretches north-south from Haarlemmerdijk to the Looiersgracht.

The name Jordaan possibly derives from the French *jardin*, when 17th-century refugee French Huguenots settled in the district which has many streets and canals named after flowers or trees: Lindenstraat, Palmstraat, Rozengracht, Bloemstraat, Leliestraat, Goudbloemstraat (Marigold Street), Egelantiersgracht (Eglantine Canal), Anjelierstraat (Carnation Street).

For a random stroll through the Jordaan, concentrate on the sector north of Bloemgracht.

Westerkerk's crown

Best starting-point is the Westerkerk (Western Church). Built 1620-38, the Westerkerk stands beside the Prinsengracht at the end of Raadhuisstraat (Town Hall Street) which runs from behind the Royal Palace on Dam Square. The 279-ft spire is the city's highest, topped by a crown of Emperor Maximilian.

The chimes of the church bells are described in the Diary of Anne Frank, who took wartime refuge with her family in a warehouse back-annexe close by on the Prinsengracht. Anne Frank's House (see chapter 6) is worth visiting early, before big crowds arrive.

The Rozengracht (Rose Canal), now filled in, is a continuation of Raadhuisstraat. Rembrandt lived his last impoverished years (1658-69) at no. 184. His model and second wife, Hendrickje Stoffels, and his son Titus also died here. Rembrandt has a memorial stone in Westerkerk, but – buried as a pauper – location of his grave is unknown.

ON FOOT
Where Rembrandt lived
Earlier, from 1631, Rembrandt's first Amsterdam home was on the Bloemgracht (Flower Canal), separated from the Rozengracht only by Bloemstraat.

In several streets you'll find delightful small almshouses. In Karthuizerstraat (Charterhouse Street), for instance, is the Huis Zitten Weduwen Hof (Widows' Almshouses), dating from 1650. Two others are in Tuinstraat – the Zeven Keurvorsten at Nos. 197-223, and the Alidaehofje.

Two more are located on Egelantiersgracht, at Nos. 50 and 111. Prinsengracht has a couple more, at Nos. 133 and 175. They all typify the care the Amsterdammers took of their old folk, and of the peace they could find in their declining years.

If you are still game for looking at old buildings, walk north to Brouwersgracht (Brewers Canal), which has some magnificent old warehouses. You'll find even more if you venture northwards beyond the Jordaan onto the small artificial island in Het IJ. They are all linked by bridges. The tiny street called Zand Hoek (Sand Corner) on their eastern side has been magnificently restored.

For a more detailed routing, ask the VVV Amsterdam Tourist Office for their walking-tour brochure called 'The Jordaan' – part of a series of six excellent itineraries. These are priced at 3.00 guilders each, and cover a 'Discovery Tour', a Maritime Walk, a Jewish Historical route, a Van Gogh Tour and a Rembrandt.

Chapter Six
Worth a visit

Amsterdam is crammed with museums, galleries and monuments. On a city break, you have to be highly selective. Below are listed the top recommendations. But there is much more scope for people with more time, or with special interests.

6.1 Buildings and Monuments

Begijnhof, The Spui
Location: Close to Amsterdam Historical Museum and Kalverstraat. Tram 1, 2, 5, 9, 16, 24, 25.

A peaceful and charming courtyard surrounded by 16th and 17th century gabled almshouses, with a small village green and church. For centuries it was a place of refuge for elderly Catholic ladies, who led a semi-religious life.

When Catholicism was banned in 1578, the church building was handed over to English Protestants and is still used by them. The resident Catholic ladies built themselves a 'concealed' church – and that, too, is still in use. The flower-filled courtyard contains one of Amsterdam's only two surviving wooden houses (the other is located at 2 Zeedijk). Building in wood was made illegal in 1521.

Heineken's Brewery, 78 Stadhouderskade
Open for several tours daily, Mon-Fri – normally three in the morning at 9.00, 9.45, and 10.30; and three in the afternoon, at 13.00, 13.45 and 14.30 hrs. Phone 523 9239 to check timings.
Location – opposite Weteringsplantsoen. Tram 16, 24, 25. Entrance fee Dfl 2, donated to charities.

SITES TO VISIT

A guided tour through the famous brewery, followed by a free beer and cheese. A very convivial atmosphere indeed! If it happens to be your birthday on the day you visit, take along your passport as proof, for a special gift.

Maximiliaan Brewery, Kloveniersburgwal 6-8, Barndesteeg 10-16 near the Nieuwmarkt.

A traditional brewery in a complex of five historical houses, features a guided tour for groups of ten or more, with a slide presentation. Tastings are offered for their three types of beer: lager, wheat beer and a dark 'triple' beer with high alcohol percentage and a spicy aftertaste.

Madame Tussaud's, 20 Dam – in the upper two floors of the Peek & Cloppenburg department store, on the corner between Kalverstraat and Rokin.
Open daily 10-17.30 hrs. **Entrance Dfl 17.50.**

Go by lift to the 4th floor, devoted entirely to daily life in Amsterdam in the 17th-century Golden Age. The showpiece is a moving panoramic view of Amsterdam. Many designs and figures are life-size 3-D versions of famous Dutch paintings.

Thence into the 20th century for wax figures of Margaret Thatcher, Marilyn Monroe, Queen Beatrix and John Major. Some figures move and talk.

Royal Palace, Dam Square
Open daily during Easter, summer and autumn holidays 12.30-16.00 hrs. Otherwise on Wed only.

See Chapter 5 for history of the Royal Palace that started as a Town Hall.

Stock Exchange building, Damrak
Open Tue-Sun 10-16 hrs. Entrance Dfl 6.00.

Amsterdam's former Stock Exchange – Beurs van Berlage – has been opened to the public since 1996, when this unusual building was exactly 100 years old. Of major architectural interest, the building is now used as a cultural centre, housing two concert halls and an impressive auction hall where temporary exhibitions take place. The tower offers magnificent views over the city.

SITES TO VISIT

6.2 Museums and Galleries

Museum entrance prices run from two guilders up to Dfl 10 for the world-famed collections. Younger age-groups and over-65's pay roughly half price. If you plan several visits to top galleries, consider buying a Museum Year-Card (Museumjaarkaart), costing Dfl 40; or Dfl 15 for under-26's; Dfl 25 for Senior Citizens.

This card gives unlimited entrance to most museums, but you still have to pay admission to temporary exhibitions. VVV offices and participating museums can sell you the card. Four entrances to major museums, and you're saving money. Otherwise, pay as you go! Specially note that several of the principal museums are closed Mondays.

Museum Amstelkring, Oude Zijds Voorburgwal 40
Location: Near Central Station, Damrak, Oude Kerk, red-light area. Open: Mon-Sat 10-17 hrs; Sun 13-17 hrs. Entrance Dfl 5.

A splendid canalside house built 1661, together with two smaller houses at the rear, preserved with the original furnishings and decoration. Across the lofts of the three houses, a 'secret' Catholic church was built – called 'Our Dear Lord in the Attic'.

Amsterdam Historical Museum, Kalverstraat 92
It is housed in a magnificent building that started as a convent dedicated to St. Lucy and was adopted as Amsterdam's municipal orphanage in 1578. Boys and girls occupied it for nearly 400 years. Open: Mon-Fri 10-17 hrs; Sat-Sun 11-17. Entry Dfl 7.50.

This fine collection, displayed with imagination, illustrates the history of Amsterdam through maps, prints, paintings and pottery, mainly 16th-20th century. Documents relate to 13th century onwards, but particularly the Museum is rich in aspects of Amsterdam's Golden Age of the 17th century.

A special bonus is entry to the Civic Guards' Gallery, a glass-roofed 'museum street' lined with massive paintings. This connects the 17th-century courtyards with the adjoining Begijnhof.

SITES TO VISIT

Anne Frank's House, Prinsengracht 263
Location: on east bank of Prinsengracht, near Westerkerk. Visit could be combined with walk around Jordaan area across the canal. Trams 13, 14, 17.
Open: Mon-Sat 9-17 hrs, Sun 10-17. From June-September, open till 19 hrs. Entrance Dfl 10.

A merchant's house, built 1635. In a secret annexe Anne Frank, a young Jewish girl, spent two years in hiding during World War II. Here she wrote her famous diary, which has been translated into 54 languages. A moving testimonial to the inhumanity of the past – a tiny fragment of world history, highlighting one young human life during the Nazi occupation.

Aviodome National Aeronautics & Spacetravel Museum, Schiphol Airport
Trains from Central Station to Schiphol Centre.
Open daily 10-17 hrs; but closed on Mondays November through to March. Entry Dfl 8.50.

A modest collection, showing development of aviation and space travel, from a 1903 Wright Brothers' contraption to the 1980's spacelab.

Electrical Museum Tramline
Great idea for the children, who have never ridden an oldtime tramcar! Operating summer weekends, vintage trams depart from 44 Karperweg, behind the Haarlemmermeerstation (reached by bus 18 from Central Station) and travel to the Amsterdamse Bos (Amsterdam Woods).

Film Museum, 3 Vondelpark
Location: north of the lake. Tram 1, 2, 5. Open Mon-Fri 10-21.30 hrs; Sat 18-21.30; Sun 12-21.30.

Library, photographs, film and posters exhibition, with film shows.

Fodor Museum, 609 Keizersgracht
Location: on Keizersgracht, between Vijzelstraat and Reguliersgracht, a short walk from Rembrandtsplein. Tram 16, 24, 25. Open daily 11-17 hrs.

Exhibitions by living Amsterdam artists, with the shows changing monthly.

SITES TO VISIT

Jewish Historical Museum (Joods Historisch Museum), 2-4 Jonas Daniel Meyerplein
Location: Close to Waterlooplein. Tram 9, 14 or Metro. Open daily 11-17 hrs. Entry Dfl 7.

The Museum, opened 1987, is based on four Ashkenazim synagogues – built in 17th and 18th centuries – which formed the heart of Jewish Amsterdam in the years before the Holocaust. This is one of Europe's most important collections of Jewish historical, religious and art-historical objects. Among the most striking features is the Sjoelgass, a glass-covered passage between the four museums providing access to the Kosher Coffee Shop.

Across the J.D. Meijerplein, which features a statue commemorating a dockers' strike in protest against Nazi treatment of the Jews, is the massive Portuguese Synagogue built in 1675 by Sephardic Jews who had earlier migrated from the Iberian peninsula.

Maritime Museum (Nederlands Scheepvaart Museum), 1 Katternburgerplein
Location: at the eastern end of Oosterdok. Bus 22, 28 from Central Station to Kadijksplein. Open Tue-Sat 10-17 hrs; Sun 13-17. Entry Dfl 12.50.

A visit is essential for anyone interested in Holland's rich seafaring history. The museum features a crowded collection of ship models across the ages, maps and paintings, navigation instruments, and all the items needed for long trading voyages to East and West Indies.

The surrounding area is likewise packed with maritime interest, including well-preserved warehouses from 17th and 18th centuries.

The building itself was formerly the Admiralty arsenal, where warships were equipped for voyages to the Far East and the Dutch West Indies. A reconstructed Dutch merchant ship, dating from Amsterdam's 17th-century Golden Age, is an attractive feature of the waterfront.

Rembrandt House, 6 Jodenbreestraat
Location: a block away from the new City Hall on Waterlooplein, close to Zwanenburgwal canal.

SITES TO VISIT

Tram 9, 14. Metro Waterlooplein.
Open Mon-Sat 10-17 hrs; Sun and holidays 13-17 hrs. Entry Dfl 7.50.

The house where Rembrandt lived from 1639-1658, until he went bankrupt and moved to a more modest dwelling in the Jordaan district.

Over 200 of his engravings and drawings are on show, and also his original etching press.

Rijksmuseum – see chapter 4.

Stedelijk Museum (Municipal Museum), 13 Paulus Potterstraat
Location: on Museum Square, next to Van Gogh Museum. Tram 2 or 5. Open daily 11-17 hrs. Entrance Dfl 10.00.

An elderly building which was given a postwar face-lift, to gain international fame for its trend-setting permanent collection of modern art from 1850 to the present day – paintings, sculptures, photos and video. The emphasis is on post-1950.

The basic collection includes works by Manet, Bonnard, Cézanne, Picasso, Matisse, Kandinsky, Chagall and Mondrian. Abstract paintings by Malevich form the largest collection of his works outside Russia.

Temporary exhibitions by living artists give every visit a touch of the unexpected. Amsterdammers themselves drop by frequently, to stay in tune with What's On in the art world.

For a mental shake-up, walk down to the basement, into the *Beanery* by American artist Edward Kienholz: a modelled Los Angeles bar with clock-faced waxwork dummies.

Theatre Museum, 168 Herengracht
Location: from Dam Square, go behind Palace, down Raadhuisstraat to Herengracht, across bridge, then right. Tram 13, 17. Open Tue-Sun 11-17 hrs. Entry Dfl 5. Check on Tel 6235104 whether yet reopened after renovation.

Ideal for theatre buffs – history of Dutch theatre, models of stage sets, temporary exhibitions – all set in one of the great houses of the 17th century.

SITES TO VISIT

Van Gogh Museum – see chapter 4.

Van Loon Museum, 672 Keizersgracht
Location: Between Reguliersgracht and Vijzelstraat, opposite Fodor Museum. Tram 16, 24, 25.
Open only on Mon 10-17 hrs and Sun 13-17 hrs. Entrance Dfl 5.

A 17th-century furnished canal house, with French-style garden.

Willet Holthuysen Museum, 605 Herengracht
Tram 4, 9. Open: daily 11-17 hrs. Entrance Dfl 5.

A canal house with authentic interior dating from 17th and 18th centuries.

Chapter Seven
Holland on day trips

7.1 Using Amsterdam as base

Amsterdam is a perfect base for seeing tourist Holland. Distances are very small, and day excursion tickets keep fares reasonable.

From Amsterdam you can easily reach Haarlem (12 miles away), blue-pottery Delft (39 miles), Aalsmeer with its Friday-morning cheese market (25 miles), The Hague (39 miles), Rotterdam (53 miles).

Another highly popular variation for City Break visitors is to take a ready-packaged coach tour – time-saving and hassle-free, with a knowledgeable guide to set the scene and answer questions. Quite apart from visiting the charming towns, coach tour circuits are routed to show the full fascination of the natural and man-made Dutch countryside.

The most popular half-day circuits are (1) Bulbfields and Keukenhof (south of Haarlem) in springtime; (2) Volendam and Marken; (3) Windmills of Zaanse Schans, and Edam, covering similar territory to the Volendam excursion, or sometimes combined with it; (4) Delft and The Hague, to include the miniature town of Madurodam, and the beach resort of Scheveningen; (5) Alkmaar cheese market, Fridays only, mid-April till mid-September.

On whole-day swings, several destinations are combined, or can include a closer look at the former Zuider Zee to the north, or Rotterdam to the south.

However limited your time, it's certainly worth picking at least one of these trips. Much of the

DAY TRIPS

North & South Holland

DAY TRIPS

countryside, waterways, villages and cities still presents a tranquil picture. Keep your eyes open in Holland, and you'll see a myriad vignettes lifted straight into the 20th century from the master paintings of the Dutch School.

Cycling

If you have the spare time and energy, seriously consider renting a bike and pedalling off into the countryside. On Amsterdam's northern doorstep – just across Het IJ – begins the Waterland district of reclaimed polder. An average-grade cyclist could easily make a day's circuit that included Broek in Waterland, Monnickendam, Marken, Volendam and Edam.

Pedalling across the pancake-flat landscape is easy, unless you hit head-winds. Most of the route, you can choose cyclists-only lanes, well marked and mapped.

7.2 Polders, cheese and windmills

Zaanse Schans

Holland's famous windmills are now few and scattered. Pumping out the canals is done more prosaically by electric power. Snap your windmill photos when you get the chance, for there won't be another dozen just as good down the road.

There's a handy solution at Zaanstad, just north of Amsterdam (10 miles away). Alongside River Zaan is the reconstructed township of Zaanse Schans which features several working windmills, including a saw-mill and a mustard mill, 17th-century green-painted houses and varied museum shops. A cheese farm and a clog-maker's workshop add to the picture of a centuries'-old working community.

Volendam

National costume is carefully preserved and encouraged in the eel-fishing villages of Volendam and Marken. Volendam was formerly a quaint fishing port which lost its main fishing income when the

DAY TRIPS

Zuyder Zee was transformed by a dyke into an inland lake.

The little harbour is crammed with fishing-boats which mainly are in the eel-catching business. Another side of the harbour is a popular centre for pleasure cruisers and yachts. Along the waterfront you can enjoy gastronomic specialties like smoked eel, or raw herrings with onion.

There are many souvenir stores lining the waterfront. But walk fifty yards down a side-street and the original charm returns, with delightful Dutch houses in a peaceful uncommercialized setting. Local people in costume are glad to keep visitors happy by posing for photographs.

Marken

Somewhat less busy is Marken – formerly a fishing village on a Zuyder Zee island, but now connected with the mainland by a road from Monnickendam that rides on top of a new dyke wall. Here was another major reclamation project – all part of the Zuyder Zee enclosure scheme that was intended to add 11% more land area to the surface of Holland. But the current policy is to call a halt to creation of still more agricultural land. Europe's butter mountain is already too high.

In Marken, the middle-aged and elderly still wear local costume without too much official encouragement. Houses are built on piles on a brick foundation, with walls of brightly-painted wood. Villagers park their painted clogs on racks beside the front door. It's a delightful spot.

Edam

Only about three miles away from Volendam is the little town of Edam, which gives its name to the most famous of Dutch cheeses.

All around is Edam-cheese territory, with spotless Dutch farmhouses. On excursions from Amsterdam, coaches usually stop for a farmhouse cheese-making demonstration, in Broek in Waterland and other neighbouring localities. It's a pleasant way of seeing something of a farmhouse interior. As a useful central-heating idea, cattle normally lived throughout winter under the same roof as the family, with winter hay stored in the loft above, to improve winter insulation even further.

But today the town of Edam itself is no longer in cheese business. It's more of an affluent dormitory town for Amsterdam. The houses and streets are a delight, dating from the 16th century. A small museum in the market square explains that, because of the high level of the groundwater, the brick-built cellar lined with tiles is actually designed to *float* like a boat. Otherwise, the upward pressure of water would cause cracks in the floors of an ordinary cellar.

It's a typical part of the problem of living below sea level!

Alkmaar
Quite apart from its world-famous cheese market, Alkmaar is a delightful town in its own right. Every Friday morning in the Weigh-House Square, 10 a.m. till midday, thousands of bright yellow cheeses are laid out, each weighing an average 12 kilos.

As buying transactions are completed, the costumed teams of the cheese carriers guild trot briskly with their loads to the 16th-century weigh-house. No fork-lift trucks on the Friday morning market! Everything follows precisely the traditions established centuries ago.

From April till October inclusive, a Cheese Museum is open Mon-Sat from 10-16 hrs in the Weigh-House building (open 9 a.m. on Fridays).

With so many visitors coming every Friday during summer, a flourishing street market offers all the traditional Dutch products – including cheese!

Formerly the cheeses were brought to the quayside by canal. That quayside is now the departure point for 45-minute boat trips that operate every 20 minutes on cheese-market days; otherwise hourly.

The former Zuyder Zee
It takes most of a whole-day trip to get a full impression of the great engineering works which converted the huge expanse of the former Zuyder Zee into the present-day freshwater Lake IJsselmeer,

The Skinny Bridge - one of Amsterdam's memorable landmarks

The cheese auction in Alkmaar - an original choice for a day trip

Cycling - a Dutch passion

Trams provide a novel way to discover the city

Brightly coloured barges line Amsterdam's famous canals

Mix with the locals in one of the convivial Brown Cafés

A souvenir of your CityBreak in Amsterdam

DAY TRIPS

thanks to building of a massive 20-mile barrier against the North Sea.

A visit can dramatically illustrate the constant battle against the sea, and to defend much of the Netherlands which lies below sea level. Since the 13th century, around 1.5 million acres of land have been reclaimed by means of dykes and drainage, with the traditional help of windmills.

Learn the sequence by which fertile polders have been created from land which formerly belonged to the North Sea. It's a fascinating story!

7.3 Bulbs and cut flowers

Bulb-fields

Late March till mid-April is season for daffodils and narcissus; and from then till mid-May for tulips and hyacinths. These dates can vary by a week, with early or late Spring. During the season, the Netherlands Board of Tourism at 18 Buckingham Gate, London SW1E 6LB can supply updated bulb-field information.

The bulb-growing districts are tightly grouped, with the best displays just south of Haarlem. The gorgeous carpets of colour attract thousands of visitors from neighbouring countries.

The main event of the Dutch bulb season is the annual *bloemencorso* – Flower Parade – usually on the last Saturday of April, but check first. Decorated floats and bands start from Haarlem in the morning and tour the bulbfields till late afternoon.

Very soon, the fields are stripped of their blooms. The industry is producing *bulbs*, not flowers. Plucking off the blooms in their prime ensures that all strength goes into the bulb.

During the bulbfield season, the highlight is 70-acre Keukenhof Park, near Lisse. Over three million tulips in 1200 varieties are displayed by commercial growers who take orders for later despatch.

From the end of March to mid-May a display of spring flowering bulbs is featured by Frans Roozen, a few miles southwest of Haarlem. Later in the year a summer show operates with gorgeous displays of summer-flowering bulbs and plants.

DAY TRIPS

Aalsmeer

If you miss the tulip season, visit Aalsmeer instead – the flower centre ten miles from Amsterdam. Daily auctions are an unforgettable sight, with carnations, roses and lilies massed by the hundred thousand ready for export around Europe.

Thanks to proximity to Schiphol Airport, with regular air freight departures mid-morning to USA, blooms can be on sale in downtown New York the same evening.

The leading auction floor is a cooperative venture of some 2,000 growers, who market their entire production through the organisation. Samples of each lot are displayed to the buyers, who then make their bids on the Dutch auction system (the price starts high, and goes down). An electronic clock – wired to a computer – halts at the price when the first buyer presses his button.

Visitors are admitted to galleries that overlook the five auction rooms where 50,000 transactions take place every working day. Go early! These Dutch auctions of cut flowers and pot plants start 7 a.m., and often finish by 10.

Afterwards, you could take a one-hour cruise along canals and around a neighbouring lake, where open stretches of water lead past little 'islands' of flower fields.

7.4 Cities to explore

Delft

A typical guide-book referred to 'the quiet beauty' of Delft, with canals 'spanned by bridges as fragile as Delft porcelain.'

Certainly, if you have the time, it's possible to recapture the atmosphere of Vermeer in a city where the canals, lime trees and sedate houses are little changed since Delft's most famous artist painted them over 300 years ago.

Meanwhile it's the fame of Delft pottery which is the main reason for a canalside halt. Visiting a pottery, with explanation of manufacture and decoration, makes an interesting interlude. (See Chapter 9 for comments on shopping for Delft porcelain).

DAY TRIPS

Haarlem

Haarlem – only a brief train ride from Amsterdam's Central Station – is worth a few hours' exploration. It has a dreamy old centre, a lively Great Market (Grote Markt) of pedestrianised shopping streets, and a splendid collection of paintings by Frans Hals and other masters of the Haarlem School.

Another ten minutes, and you can reach the beach resort of Zandfoort.

The Hague

The Hague - seat of Dutch Government and of the International Court of Justice - is a sedate city, solid and prosperous from the great days of the Dutch Empire.

In the centre is the Vijver – a stately lake with swans floating serenely – and the Binnenhof, a historic group of buildings where the present-day Dutch parliament meets.

A Binnenhof conducted tour lasts almost an hour – a colour-slide presentation of the background history, with four-language commentary through ear-phones; then a visit to the glorious 13th-century Ridderzaal where the state opening of the parliament takes place every September. The wooden roof of Irish oak is a masterpiece of craftsmanship.

Through a gateway, you reach the Mauritshuis – originally a patrician mansion, but now used as a small and elegant art gallery that contains some of the the world's greatest treasures. Over a dozen Rembrandts include several self-portraits and the world-famed 'Anatomy Lesson'.

There are numerous paintings by Rubens, Jan Steen, Vermeer, van Dyck, Holbein and Frans Hals. Unlike so many of Europe's great galleries, you are not overwhelmed by the sheer volume of canvasses.

Scheveningen

Virtually a suburb of The Hague is Scheveningen, Holland's principal seaside resort, with miles of fine sand, safe but cool bathing, and all the usual beach amenities. The fishing village is delightful, with women dressed in photogenic local costume.

DAY TRIPS

Madurodam

Opened near Scheveningen in 1950 is the miniature town of Madurodam which reproduces many of the Holland's historic buildings in 1/25th scale. It's not just for children! Outside the school holidays, adults far outnumber the under-14's.

Faithful reproductions give a close-up view of the architecture and layout of city centres and market towns. It's also of great appeal to model railway enthusiasts, who can visit the control room with lights to indicate how the system works.

On the road back to Amsterdam, some tours pass through Wassenaar, which has millionaires' houses, some with thatched roofs. In the local hotel, Eisenhower stayed for six weeks immediately after the War.

Rotterdam

The entire centre of Rotterdam – Holland's leading port – was demolished by German bombing on the 3rd May 1940. Since then, the centre has been totally rebuilt. In contrast to the traditional architecture of most other Dutch cities, Rotterdam is ultra-modern.

Some of the architecture – such as an apartment block with cube-shaped rooms apparently tilted and balanced on their points – has aroused great controversy. But many of the commercial buildings – like the superb World Trade Centre, of curved green glass – have much greater appeal.

A dramatic and anguished monument commemorates the wartime destruction, and puts across the message: "Please, no more bombings! Because Rotterdam lost its heart – lost its centre."

Chapter Eight
Architectural delight

8.1 The making of Amsterdam

In the beginning there was just water and mud, a swampy area between Amstel River and the old Zuyder Zee. Fishermen settled there and built a dam to protect their tiny village from the sea.

They named their hamlet after the river and the dam: Amstelledamme – so called in the earliest surviving document, dated 1275, when the community had prospered enough to be granted a city charter.

From that time onwards, Amsterdam's archives contain details of virtually all building work. The documents are so complete that it's often possible to take engravings 400 or 500 years old, and name the original owners of every house in the picture. The Amsterdam Historical Museum traces the town's development in great detail. History buffs can visit the Archives.

Amsterdam's medieval layout is reflected in surviving street or canal names. As fishermen, selling their catch to markets deep inland, the citizens of Amsterdam needed salt for curing, and wood for barrels. So they sailed to the Baltic for timber, and to Portugal for salt.

Today, close to the original dam which is now Dam Square, is Zoutsteeg (*zout* means salt) where the salt cargoes were unloaded. The lines of city walls are marked by Nieuwezijds Voorburgwal, and Oudezijds Voorburgwal and Achterburgwal (burgwal means city wall). The sea defences were completed by the Zeedijk (Sea dyke).

ARCHITECTURE

City planning

Originally Amsterdam houses were built of wood. In 1421, one-third of the town was destroyed by fire. Some thirty years later, three-quarters of the town was destroyed. So, in the 15th century the town council decreed that the walls of all houses should be of brick. Today there are only two wooden houses left in the city.

By the early 17th century, the town's trading prosperity had outgrown the original city limits, marked by the Singel (meaning Belt or Girdle) which had acted as the west-side moat.

Bursting at the girdle, but hemmed in by the soggy subsoil, the city fathers in 1612 started on an ambitious development programme. That was the period when the main crescent-shaped belt of concentric canals – Herengracht (Gentlemen's Canal), Keizersgracht (Emperor's Canal), and Prinsengracht (Princes' Canal) – was laid out in classic town planning style.

It was all custom-built to serve the needs of the 'Gentlemen', the wealthy merchants who gave the town its extraordinary prosperity in the 17th century. The three main canals were designed to bring boats right to the doorsteps of the warehouse-homes that lined them. A final canal girdle was added, called Singelgracht.

More expansion

Then, 19th century, came a fresh wave of expansion outside the Singelgracht. In that period the Leidseplein was developed, together with Vondelpark and the Rijksmuseum.

The waterway leading up to Dam Square was filled in, to become the Damrak. And an artificial island was created in Het IJ, on which today's Central Station is located.

During the 20th century, Amsterdam has spread further out – but always in a tidy, city-planned style.

Meanwhile, the basic layout from medieval times and the 17th-century has remained unchanged – a key factor that explains the supreme charm of Amsterdam today.

ARCHITECTURE

8.2 Looking at buildings

There was a touch of genius about Amsterdam's 17th-century exercise in town planning. The finest of the handsome red-brick houses were built for very wealthy Gentlemen and merchants on the insider-canal, Herengracht.

Next in the pecking order was Keizersgracht, more middle-class. The artisan outsiders, and their workshops, were located mainly on the outer ring, the Princes' Canal.

Each of the canals was lined with a beautiful avenue of trees, which still flourish. Every house sits on piles, 14 to 60 feet long, driven into the firmer sand beneath the upper stratum of loam and loose sand. Remember that most of Amsterdam is below sea level.

The merchant lifestyle

The merchants, instead of living 'over the shop' preferred to live under the warehouse. Costly goods and spices imported from the Far East were stored on top floors, above the living quarters and offices, safe from damp and burglars.

Every house was fitted with a hoist, pulley and tackle, protruding from the loft. Goods unloaded from the canalside were then hauled up for storage. Even in modern times, on moving day, furniture goes in and out the big picture windows: much better than struggling with a grand piano up the steep staircases.

With canal frontage so precious, taxation was based on the *width* of houses. Houses were built narrow but very tall to make best use of the prime building lots, standardised at around 30 feet frontage with depth of 190 feet.

Back development into the rear gardens gave much greater depth and living-space than seems possible from the narrow facades.

A few wealthy citizens could afford a double plot. Occasionally, two families – brothers, for instance – would combine to build a more imposing double-width facade, with the architect planning for two individual houses within.

ARCHITECTURE

Luxury interiors

However, most houses were built to the standard 30-ft width, with a family's wealth reflected in the luxury status symbols of domestic interiors: high-quality furniture, rich tapestries, Venetian glass, Turkish carpets, and paintings that kept innumerable Dutch artists constantly busy.

The narrow house exteriors gave relatively little scope for embellishment – apart from the gable ends, where imagination ran riot. Fashion played its part. Step gables were in vogue mainly throughout the 17th century and until around 1750 when they gave way to the simplified spout gable. Step gables were a characteristic styling of the city's master-architect, Hendrick de Keyser, who built several Protestant churches and many private houses.

Decorative gables

Also popular from mid-17th century were the neck and bell gables, much more elaborate and whimsical. Gable ornamentation had free rein: heraldic devices, trade emblems, every neighbour a different oddity. These facades served to identify an address, in the days before houses were numbered. Take a long-focus lens, to capture some of the details!

Some 7,000 buildings in central Amsterdam are protected by preservation orders. Likewise, whenever possible, canal bridges have been restored to their original state. On a canal trip by night, new scenes open up. Many of the locals don't pull their curtains in the evening, so you get delightful vignettes of domestic interiors.

Stately mansions have been divided into flats, except where rents are so high that only banks and insurance companies can afford the price. Eighty per cent of Amsterdam housing is rented.

Hence the postwar phenomenon of houseboat living. Owing to accommodation shortage, living on the water became the only solution for many people. Some 2,400 houseboats are moored along the canals. Half of them are registered, and are linked to gas, electricity and water services. The others do not have these facilities. But mostly the interiors are as impeccable as those ashore.

Chapter Nine

Go shopping

9.1 Browsing around the shops

Anyone who enjoys shopping will find endless potential in Amsterdam. Among the principal shopping streets are Damrak, Kalverstraat, Leidsestraat and P.C. Hoofstraat. But there are also many trendy little shops between the girdle of canals, and in the Jordaan. Thanks to Holland's low inflation rate you get value for money, but no great bargains.

Shop-gazing is a Dutch pastime, so don't worry about being pressed by sales staff, who are invariably good humoured and courteous. Don't forget to visit the markets, which are full of character and offer a wide selection. Wear flat shoes as the cobbled streets are a nightmare in high heels.

Shop hours are generally:

Mon	13.00 – 18.00 hrs
Tue, Wed, Fri	09.00 – 18.00 hrs
Thu	09.00 – 21.00 hrs
Sat	09.00 – 17.00 hrs

Schiphol Duty-Free

A final shopping-tip: give yourself ample spare time on departure from Amsterdam Airport, to explore the Duty-Free Stores. You can buy watches, photo and electronic equipment, binoculars, perfume and the usual cigarettes and liquor – often at lower prices than in the countries of origin.

Flowers are top quality and well packed, and will arrive fresher at your destination than if bought in town. However, foodstuffs like cheese, herring and waffles are more expensive than in supermarkets.

SHOPPING

9.2 The main shopping areas

Kalverstraat and the Rokin

At a turning off Dam Square is a pedestrian precinct called Kalverstraat. The most famous shopping street of Amsterdam, Kalverstraat features all the Dutch specialties – Edam cheese, porcelain, pewter, crystal, silverware, handicrafts and antiques.

Here you'll get a square deal at reasonable prices, with honest shipping of loot that's too heavy to carry around.

A parallel street is Rokin, which goes more for high fashion, jewellers, art galleries and luxury antiques.

Leidsestraat

Shops line the entire route, traffic-free except for bicycles and trams. Aim to finish at Leidseplein, to reward yourself with a drink at a café on the square.

Muntplein to Rembrandtsplein

Good daytime shopping, and you can make a mental note of restaurants and bars for evening entertainment. Also look at Reguliersbreestraat and Utrechtsestraat.

Museum Quarter

An up-market shopping area along P.C. Hoofstraat and Van Baerlestraat – located between Museum Square and the entrance to Vondelpark.

The Spiegel Quarter

Here's a heavy concentration of top-grade antique dealers – 80 of them, and 15 galleries, in a 300-metre line-up along Nieuwe Spiegelstraat, which runs from opposite the Rijksmuseum across Prinsengracht, Keizersgracht and through to Herengracht.

The area is sheer joy to serious collectors, with choice of enough antiquities to fill a museum. But the prices are set by specialist dealers who know precisely the value of their stock! You'll certainly need a well-padded credit card to go shopping here.

SHOPPING

9.3 Department Stores

De Bijenkorf, 90 Damrak – rated as Amsterdam's most fashionable and well-stocked store, with cafés and lunch-rooms on each floor. Try their self-service lunch.

Maison de Bonneterie, 140 Rokin backing on to 183 Kalverstraat – renovated turn-of-the-century elegance with chandeliers. Bargain sales in July and August.

Marks & Spencer, 66-72 Kalverstraat – three floors of English quality goods which are probably cheaper in UK. But the take-away sandwiches are good value and locally produced.

Metz & Co., 455 Keizersgracht – claimed as Europe's oldest department store, founded in 1740. Go to the top floor for a great panorama of Amsterdam. Sales in July-August.

Vroom & Dreesman, 201 Kalverstraat – the Amsterdam branch of a leading Dutch chain.

Magna Plaza Shopping Centre

Located on the Nieuwezijds Voorburgwal, immediately behind the Royal Palace, Magna Plaza is a stunning 1990's reconstruction of the former Central Post Office, which was a monument of 1898 architecture. The original fanciful facade has been totally preserved.

Go to enjoy the light-hearted 'Gothic/Moorish' style of the interior decor, which is designed to put customers in the mood for 'fun shopping'.

There are pleasant seating areas for refreshments, snacks and light meals. The shopping centre features dozens of trendy clothing and leisure-related stores: from music, sport and hobbies, to fashion, toys and travel.

Virgin occupies a prime corner of the ground floor and much of the basement, but there are few bargains.

SHOPPING

9.4 Street Markets

There's delight in Amsterdam's selection of 26 street markets, full of atmosphere and colour. Here's a short list:

Antique Market 'De Looier', Elandsgracht 109
Tram 7, 10, 14. Open Mon-Thu 11-17; Sat 9-17.
Close to the Jordaan district, this indoor antique market sells a wide range of collectibles of doubtful quality.

Bird Market, Noordermarkt
Saturday morning only.

Book Market, Spui
Tram 1, 2, 5. Friday 7-17 hrs only.
Bookstalls offer new and second-hand books, including some English-language, in an area of cafés and bookshops. A Sunday art market operates 10-18 hrs, April till end of November.

Book Market, Oudemanhuispoort
Walking distance from Muntplein, or the Rokin end of Spui. Open Mon-Sat 11-16 hrs.
A narrow passage in the vicinity of the University of Amsterdam, the market is a pleasant hunting-ground for students in search of second-hand academic tomes, while others browse for postcards, posters and antiquarian books.

Flea Market, Waterlooplein
Tram 9, 14. Open Mon-Sat 10-17 hrs.
To connoisseurs of flea markets, this one gets high rating: everything guaranteed second-hand, from rusty tools to old books, postcards, prints, you-name-it.

Flower Market, Singel
Tram 1, 2, 5. Open Mon-Sat 9-18 hrs.
Europe's only floating flower market, along the Singel Canal between Muntplein and Koningsplein. Take your camera to capture the dazzling colours.

SHOPPING

General Market, Albert Cuypstraat
Tram 4, 16, 24, 25. Open Mon-Fri 9-18 hrs; Sat 9-17 hrs.
A mile-long pedestrian precinct, comprising Amsterdam's largest open-air food market. Sample the Dutch specialty of herring with onions!

General Market, Lindengracht
Saturday morning only.

Stamp Market, facing no. 280 Nieuwezijds Voorburgwal
Tram 1, 2, 5. Open Wed and Sat 13-16 hrs.
Selling coins and stamps, the stall-holders compete with local philatelic shops.

Art Market, Thorbeckeplein
Tram 4, 9, 16, 24, 25. Sundays 11-18 hrs, April till October.
Every type of art and craft in this square, surrounded by cafés and restaurants.

9.5 Buying the Dutch specialities

For mementoes of your holiday in Holland, it's fun to buy direct from producers, with the chance of seeing production first-hand.

Bulbs
During the springtime bulbfield season, commercial growers have sales stands at Keukenhof Park, and also at roadside greenhouses. When a particular variety takes your fancy, you can give your order for later despatch - usually about October. You can also place an order for your spring bulbs from Franz Roozen.

If you buy bulbs, pot-plants or flowers – at the Singel flower market, for instance – remember that there are Plant Health controls on imports into Britain. The concessionary limits for returning travellers are 2 kilos of bulbs, a bouquet of cut flowers, plus 5 house plants (but not bonsai trees, dahlias or chrysanthemums).

SHOPPING

Clogs

Clogs are still worn in country districts, as practical footwear for muddy fields. But far more are produced for the tourist trade. However, Dutch townfolk themselves often buy brightly-painted clogs, hanging them on a wall as decorative holders for plants.

If you're buying clogs to wear, be sure of a loose fit with space for a finger at the heel, to avoid chafing.

A visit to a clog-maker's workshop is usually included on sightseeing coach tours that go from Amsterdam to Zaanse Schans. It's fascinating to watch a craftsman rough out clogs with the help of a 'copying lathe', from blocks of willow-tree wood to a product ready for decoration.

Cheese

In Edam-cheese territory, most of the familiar yellow and red 'cannon-balls' are made in modern factories. But a few farmhouses demonstrate the traditional cheese-making techniques. Farm-made cheeses always carry a square label.

How old is the cheese? Age has a big influence on flavour. A young cheese is reckoned as 4 weeks old; slightly matured is 8 weeks; matured cheese is 4 months old; extra matured, 7 months; old cheese is 10 months; aged cheese is one year.

Cheesemakers advise you to keep cheese in a cool pantry, *not* in a fridge. When you cut into an Edam cheese, smear the exposed area with butter, to prevent the surface drying out.

Porcelain

Want to buy some Blue Delft? Most of the so-called delftware sold in souvenir stores is mass produced in northern Holland, in the province of Friesland; or is imported from numerous countries, including Taiwan. Some is labelled as 'hand-painted in Delft blue colour'.

Only one original porcelain factory still remains in Delft – De Porceleyne Fles, founded 1653. You can visit their showrooms, where potters' wheel and painting demonstrations are given.

Another Delft pottery that continues the traditions is de Delftse Pauw, in a canalside location. Models for vases and plates derive from three centuries ago.

If you're looking for genuine Delft, check the trade mark which differentiates between real and imitation, and ask for a certificate of authenticity.

In Amsterdam, you can see pottery being painted at the Prinsengallery at Prinsengracht 440.

Diamonds

No free samples, but diamond cutting firms are glad to show you the process which has made Amsterdam so world-famed in cutting and polishing. To connoisseurs, 'Amsterdam cut' is a synonym for excellence – a tradition that has lasted since 1586, when craftsmen moved here from Antwerp.

Sightseeing tours of Amsterdam normally include a diamond-factory visit in the itinerary, but with no obligation or pressure to buy. Partly, the factories regard these tours as helping to promote the industry, reminding the world that diamonds are still a girl's best friend.

If you do feel tempted, Amsterdam's prices are claimed to be among the lowest in the world. For those who live outside the European Community, diamonds can be bought tax-free.

Sales staff advise about the 'four C's' – colour, clarity, cut and carat.

Purchases come with a guarantee certificate of the gem-stone's characteristics. Diamond-cutting and polishing demonstrations are available at the following factories:

Amsterdam Diamond Centre, Rokin 1.
Bonebakker, Rokin 88.
Coster Diamonds, Paulus Potterstraat 2.
Samuel Gassan Diamond House, Nieuwe Uilenburgerstraat 173/175.
Bab Hendriksen Diamonds, Weteringschans 89.
Holhuysen-Stoeltie B.V., Wagenstraat 13.
The Mill Diamond Centre, Rokin 123.
Van Moppes Diamonds, Albert Cuypstraat 2.
River Diamonds Centre, Weteringschans 79.

SHOPPING

Silverware and pewter

Dutch craftsmen have good reputation for silver workmanship, with quality guaranteed by a hallmark system. Antique pieces are stamped with the Amsterdam seal, and alloys are marked with a lion standing or rampant.

Modern styles of silver craftsmanship reflect the main themes of Dutch tourism, from windmills to miniature clogs. Silver filigree work originated from Indonesia.

Another thriving industry is based on pewter, with a wide range of flower vases and pewter tankards which make good souvenirs or presents.

Sweets

Chocolate is a Dutch speciality, with a high reputation for quality. If you have a sweet tooth, try Droste, Verkade or Van Houten – these are all very good brands.

Liquorice or 'dropjes' is another favourite, appearing in all shapes and sizes, both sweet and salty.

Chapter Ten
Eating out

10.1 Dutch cuisine

As a sturdy nation of cyclists, with substantial waistlines to support, the Dutch don't believe in finicky eating. A standard Dutch breakfast may include different types of bread, slices of cheese, ham, jam or honey.

That's enough to keep people going until 11 a.m. - time for coffee with a doorstep of currant bread, covered in thickly sliced butter. The Dutch do their daily best to reduce the dairy mountain.

They are then all set until the midday snack: maybe a Dutch pancake one foot two inches across; or an *uitsmijter*, buttered bread and ham, with fried eggs perched on the summit.

Another lunchtime favourite is *Koffietafel*. This comprises several types of bread, including currant loaf, a plate of cheese, sliced cold meats, butter and plentiful coffee. Sometimes *Koffietafel* also includes a bowl of thick pea-soup, or a hot croquette.

Then there's nothing more to eat until it's time for five o'clock gin with *bitterballen*, fried meat balls. Meanwhile, anyone feeling the call of hunger can pause at a wayside stall or delicatessen for a *broodje*. That's a bread roll, filled with anything from cheese or cooked meat to varied seafood like herring, kipper, smoked eel, salmon, crab or shrimp.

If something sweeter is preferred, specialist pancake houses offer a long list of flavours, sweet or savoury. A typical small pancake costs 3.50 guilders, medium size Dfl 6, and large Dfl 9. Liqueurs

EATING OUT

come extra – Dutch orange liqueur, for instance. Three pancakes could put you over the limit. Waffles (*stoopwafels*) come doused in maple syrup.

Anyone still feeling hungry and thirsty can try another Dutch institution called the *eetcafé*. That's a café with the normal range of drinks, but also a basic choice of bar food. Often the menu is chalked on a blackboard, and can include several 'specialties of the day'.

All these light-snack possibilities help the Hollanders to survive till six p.m., when it's time for the Dutch to have dinner, claimed to be their first proper meal of the day.

Certainly there is good choice of eating in Amsterdam, from a simple sandwich-lunch to an extensive five-course dinner by candlelight. There are restaurants that feature typically Dutch dishes, and countless others that enable you to dine 'in any language' – French, Italian, Spanish, Greek, Japanese, you-name-it.

For a leisured dinner, try one of Amsterdam's many Indonesian restaurants, which have added a fascinating touch of the Orient to local eating habits: a heritage of 300 years of Dutch colonialism. Incidentally, to the Dutch, Chinese means Indonesian, so far as food is concerned.

Rijsttafel

Top specialty is *rijsttafel*, probably the best value in town. Around a foundation of rice, you help yourself to platters of mysterious spicy foods that are placed by the dozen on your table. Here's a typical selection provided by the Manchurian Restaurant.

First came cold starter dishes of cabbage, sweet and sour cucumber, potato chips, coconut, prawn crackers, fried banana and peanuts. Then came the hot dishes: sweet beef, spicy beef, green beans in Bali sauce, cabbage and carrot, bean sprout and peppers, Sate (like a kebab) with peanut butter sauce, meatballs, curried chicken, and chicken egg in spicy sauce.

Tighten your belt all day, otherwise you'll never make it! Normally there's no room left for dessert – just coffee and hot towels.

EATING OUT

Warning: some of the spices are so hot, they'll set your throat on fire. Have a glass of beer or water handy, to put out the flames. Or gulp some rice or vegetables, to absorb the heat. However, many restaurants modify the full impact by using more sugar and coconut in their recipes.

Finally, don't pick a restaurant at random, which could leave you with tummy problems. Get a local recommendation, or choose from restaurants listed in the following pages.

A blue TOURIST MENU sign with an upright fork is displayed by restaurants that provide a 3-course menu priced at an all-inclusive price. Some 500 restaurants throughout Holland participate, and a complete list of addresses is available from tourist information offices.

An alternative emblem is 'NEERLANDS DIS' with a tureen displayed on a yellow background, indicating a restaurant with Dutch home cooking, offering good choice of original Dutch and/or regional specialties. These restaurants are moderately expensive.

For a snack between meals, try eating open-air at a herring stall. The Dutch say they learnt the art of preparing herrings from the English. But they've made it peculiarly their own.

There's nothing like swallowing a quick selection of *zoet* (sweet) and *zuur* (sour) herring and a *rolmops* or two at a herring stall near Central Station – particularly if you can then migrate to a friendly bar and wash the herring down with a glass or two of *jenever* (Dutch gin).

You may prefer the other extreme – somewhere with elegant setting and smooth service; or a cosy dive, made for relaxation; or an ethnic setting with exotic food; or a cheerful, noisy place with easygoing atmosphere. Amsterdam has them all.

A few final points
- You may find that restaurants display 2 menus – one for full meals, and the other 'small menu' for snacks and dishes of the day.
- English menus are nearly always available.

EATING OUT

- Service is always included in the price, though it's customary to leave a tip.
- In a normal Dutch restaurant, helpings are huge. If you order both the starter and the main course, you'll never have room left for dessert. In fact, if you start with a traditional pea soup – *erwtensoep* – you'll even find it hard to struggle through main course!

The Dutch say *eet smakelijk* – 'enjoy your meal'.

10.2 Restaurant guide

Price range

To help you decide where to eat we have categorised restaurants into different types of cuisine and indicated the approximate cost of meal by the symbols below.

Symbol	Approximate amount
£	under £10
££	£10-£20
£££	£20+

Restaurants

Within each category you can eat for as much or as little as you chooce. Here are a few of the restaurants you may enjoy. But Amsterdam has many more.

Dutch cuisine

De Eenhorn, 6 tweede Elegantiersdwarsstraat
 Tel: 623 83 52. Open 17-23 hrs, daily.   ££
A restaurant popular with the locals in the Jordaan area, with terrace open in summer. Wide variety of Dutch food.

Haesje Claes, 320 Nieuwe Zijds Voorburgwal
 Tel: 624 99 98. Open 12.00-22.00 hrs daily.   ££
A top recommendation for this charming restaurant in a narrow-frontage building dating from 1520. Excellent traditional food in a convivial atmosphere. Tourist menu available.

EATING OUT

Old Dutch Inn, Zoutsteeg (an alley near C & A's on Damrak) £
Basically a brown café, very central, with good selection of pancakes.

Holland Village, Oudezijdskolk 55 ££
Tel: 624 18 76. Open 12-15 and 18.00-23.30 hrs. Evening folklore shows with typical Dutch meal.

Die Port van Cleve, 178-180 Nieuwe Zijds Voorburgwal. Tel: 624 00 47. ££
This large Dutch-style dining hall behind the Royal Palace has been serving substantial meals since 1870. Try their thick pea soup and a steak.

Indonesian cuisine

Sama Sebo, 27 PC Hoofstraat
Tel: 662 81 46. 12.00-15.00 and 18.00-22.00 hrs, closed Sundays ££
A famous restaurant, favoured by businessmen for lunch. Choose from a variety of set menus, with big helpings. Reservations necessary.

Manchurian, 10a Leidseplein
Tel: 623 13 30. Open 12.00-15.00 and 17.00-23.00 hrs daily. ££
Selection of excellent rijsttafels, but is also fully equipped for Chinese cuisine – Cantonese, Pekin and Szechwan – Vietnamese and Thai.

Sea Palace, 8 Oosterdokskade
Tel: 626 47 77. Open 12-23 hrs daily. ££
Very large floating restaurant, specialising in Chinese food but also serves rijsttafel. Beautiful decor. Try to book a window seat.

Romantic

La Camargue, 7 Reguliersdwarsstraat
Tel: 623 93 52. Open 17.30-22.00 hrs daily. £££
Cosy, romantic restaurant. They specialise in game during the season, September onwards through winter – wild boar, hare and venison.

EATING OUT

International Menus

Kelderhof, 494 Prinsengracht
Tel: 622 06 82. Open 17.30-23.00 hrs daily. £££
Excellent French specialities. Set in a reconstructed south European courtyard and accompanied by South American guitarists on some evenings.

Les Quatre Papillons, Beulingstraat 5-7 (behind Koningsplein) Tel: 626 19 12
Open 12-14 daily except Sun 18-23 hrs. ££
An intimate restaurant with French charm.

Steak Houses

El Rancho, 3 Spui
Tel: 625 67 64. Open 12.00-24 hrs daily. £
A lively restaurant, part of a chain. Tourist menu.

Los Gauchos, 45 Korte Leidsedwarsstraat
Tel: 623 80 87. Open 17-24.00 hrs daily. ££
Excellent Argentinian food in a wood-and-leather decorated room. Serenaded by traditional song.

Piet de Leeuw, 11 Noorderstraat
Tel: 623 71 81. Open 12-22 hrs daily. ££
A steak house which also has good reputation for its beef casseroles.

Café Klos, Kerkstraat 41
Tel: 625 37 30. Open 17.30-23.30 hrs daily. ££
The best spare ribs in town! No reservations.

Mexican cuisine

Rose's Cantina, 38 Regulierdwarsstraat
Tel: 625 97 97. Open 17.30-23.00 hrs daily. ££
Tacos, tortillas and typical Mexican dishes in a lively and crowded atmosphere. Reservations not possible. Be prepared for a long wait!

Alfonso's, Korte Leidsedwarsstraat 69
Tel: 627 05 80. Open 12-24 hrs daily. ££
Young, lively atmosphere.

EATING OUT

Very Special and Expensive

All of these restaurants are elegant and rated among the best in Amsterdam for good food and service.

Dynasty, 30 Regulierdwarsstraat
 Tel: 626 84 00. Open 17.30-23.00 hrs, closed Tue. £££
Chinese restaurant, in the same group as the Manchurian – see above. Highest rating for its Thai and Cantonese food.

Le Pêcheur, 32 Regulierdwarsstraat
 Tel: 624 31 21. Open 12-15 & 18-23 hrs daily, but no lunch Sat or Sun. £££
Elegant restaurant, rated among the best in Amsterdam for fish.

Kersentuin, Dijsselhofplantsoen 7
 Tel: 664 21 21. Open 12.00-14.30 & 18.00-22.30 hrs Mon-Fri; 18.00-22.30 Sat. £££
International cuisine.

't Swarte Schaep, 24 Korte Leidsedwarsstraat
 Tel: 622 30 21. Open 12.00-23.00 hrs daily. £££
Classic French cuisine at "The Black Sheep", on the first floor of a building dating from 1687. Top quality, and courteous service. The wine list goes to 60 pages.

Japanese cuisine

Yamazoto, Hotel Okura, Ferdinand Bolstraat 333
 Tel: 678 71 11. Open 12.00-14.30 & 18.30-22.00 hrs daily. £££
Traditional Japanese cuisine, in a Japanese-operated hotel which also features a sushi bar and a teppanyaki steak house.

Yoichi, 128 Weteringschans
 Tel: 622 68 29. Open 18-23 hrs. Closed Mon.£££
Basic Dutch decor, but serving authentic Japanese food.

EATING OUT

Kyo, 2a Jan Luykenstraat
 Tel: 671 69 16. Open 18-23 hrs. Closed Sun. £££
Choose from various set menus. You can book a table in the Japanese room and sit on the floor if you wish.

Small and Inexpensive

't Balkje, 46 Kerkstraat
 Tel: 622 05 66. Open 10-20 hrs daily. £
A vast range of snacks and sandwiches to try, and good value for money.

De Gijsbrecht van Aemstel, 435 Herengracht
 Open 12-23 hrs Mon-Sat. £
Good variety of small snacks, soups and fish. Lots of character in this former stable.

Pancake Houses

The Pancake Bakery, 191 Prinsengracht
 Tel: 625 13 33. Open 12.00-21.30 hrs daily. £
Rustic pancake house.

Panne Koekhuis, 358 Prinsengracht
 Tel: 622 36 28. Open 12.00-20.30 hrs, Wed-Sun only. £
Authentic and cosy.

Fast Food Outlets
All these are easily spotted in Amsterdam – ideal for quick snacks whilst shopping, or in between morning and afternoon excursions. £

McDonalds – Pizzaland – Burger King – Kentucky Fried Chicken – FEBO Automats £

Vegetarian

Golden Temple, Utrechtstraat 126
 Tel: 626 85 60. Open 17-21 hrs daily. ££
Excellent salad bar, and good choice of natural baked products.

EATING OUT

10.3 Typical Dutch snacks

Broodje Fresh bread rolls served with a large variety of very generous fillings. A particularly popular variety is the 'half om' which is made half with ham and half with thinly sliced cooked liver.

Uitsmijter This translates loosely as 'bouncer' or 'thrower-out' and, as the story goes, was served to sober up serious imbibers before returning home to their wives. It consists of slices of bread and cheese with ham or roast beef and topped with 2 or 3 fried eggs.

Erwtensoep Traditional thick Dutch pea soup with slices of ham or sausage – a meal in itself.

Bitterballen A great Dutch favourite – spiced meat balls fried in breadcrumbs and served hot. These are often eaten with an aperitif served in most bars.

Pannekoeken/Poffertjes Pancakes served in real pancake houses. Particularly delicious are those with chopped apples, ginger or syrup.

Haring A delicacy in Holland – special raw herring served with raw chopped onions.

Paling Smoked eel – usually served on toast.

Liquorice Or 'drop' as it is known here – this can be found in abundance, either sweet or salty and in an endless variety of shapes and sizes.

Appelgebak met slagroom Open spicy apple pie with lots of cinammon and whipped cream.

EATING OUT
Febo Shops
Offering automatic fast food from vending machines. You are presented with a row of small drawers from which you choose. There are all types of slot-machine hamburgers, croquettes and cheese puffs.

Also try from the counter 'frites speciales' a box of chips with mayonnaise or tomato ketchup and finely chopped raw onions.

Pastries and Chocolates
The best place in town is Errol Trumpie's for strong Dutch coffee or cream teas and naughty cakes. Their window display of chocolates is a mouthwatering feast.

Errol Trumpie's is at Leidsestraat 46, open Mon-Sat 9-17 hrs; Sun 11-17 hrs.

10.4 Guide to the menu

Soups and Starters

Edammer kaaskroketten	Edam cheese croquettes
Garnalen	Shrimps
Gebonden soep	Cream soup
Heldere soep	Consomme
Hollandse bruine bonen soep	Dutch kidney-bean soup
Kalfsvlees pasteitjes	Veal vol-au-vent
Ossestaart soep	Oxtail soup
Russisch ei	Russian egg salad
Salade bokaal	Salad bowl
Uiensoep	Onion soup

Main courses and snacks

Biefstuk	Steak
Bitterballen	Spicy deep-fried meatballs
Boerenomelet	Farmer's omelette
Capucijners met spek	Marrow-fat peas with bacon

EATING OUT

Ei	Egg
Forel	Trout
Gehakte biefstuk	Steak tartare
Gebakken mosselen	Fried mussels
Gekookte mosselen	Steamed mussels
Gegrilde vleessoorten	Mixed grill
Gerookte zalm	Smoked salmon
Gerookte paling	Smoked eel
Ham	Ham
Hutspot	A stew of beef, potatoes, onions and carrots
Kaas	Cheese
Kotelet	Chop
Koud vlees	Cold meat
Lamsvlees	Lamb
Omelet met ham	Ham omelette
Omelet met kaas	Cheese omelette
Omelette Rolpens	Minced beef, fried apples and red cabbage
Rosbief Sandwich	Roast beef open sandwich
Sate	Small kebabs smothered in a tangy peanut-butter sauce
Scholfilet	Fillet of flounder
Spek	Bacon
Stampot	Cabbage with smoked sausage
Stampot boerenkool	Hotch-potch of curly kale
Tong filets	Fillets of sole
Varkensvlees	Pork
Varkenshaasje	Pork Fillet
Vleeskroketten	Meat croquettes
Vis	Fish
Vis uit de Rokerij	Assorted smoked fish
Warme vlees	Hot sliced beef
Worst	Sausage
Zuurkool met spek en worst	Sauerkraut, bacon and sausage

EATING OUT

Vegetables

Aardappelen	Potatoes
Boerenkool	Kale
Bruin bonen	Kidney beans
Capucijners	Marrow-fat peas
Champignons	Mushrooms
Doperwten	Peas
Gebakken aardappelen	Fried potatoes
Groente	Vegetables
Knoflook	Garlic
Pommes frites	French fried potatoes
Prei	Leek
Rijst	Rice
Sla	Salad
Tomaten	Tomatoes
Uien	Onions
Witte boon	Butter bean

Desserts

Ananas	Pineapple
Ijs	Ice-cream
Kinderysje	Children's ice-cream
Kaasplateau met stokbrood	Cheese board with french bread
Rumrozijnpudding	A thick, cream custard studded with raisins and laced with rum, which is often served with ice-cream or in hot pancakes
Slagroom	Cream
Vanille ijs	Vanilla ice-cream
Verse fruit salade	Fresh fruit salad
Vruchten	Fruit salad

Drinks

Appelsap	Apple juice
Bier	Beer
Koffie	Coffee
Koffie met slagroom	Coffee with cream

EATING OUT

Limonade	Lemonade
Melk	Milk
Mineraal water	Mineral water
Sinaasappelsap	Orange juice (usually freshly squeezed)
Thee	Tea
Thee met citroen	Lemon tea
Tomatensap	Tomato Juice
Wijn	Wine ('rood' is red and 'wit' is white)
Warme chocolademelk (met slagroom)	Hot chocolate (with cream)
Water	Water

Miscellaneous

Appelmoes	Apple sauce
Boter	Butter
Chocolade	Chocolate
Honing	Honey
Ijs	Ice
Jam	Jam
Marmelade	Marmalade
Mayonaise	Mayonnaise
Noot	Nut
Peper	Pepper
Pindakaas	Peanut butter
Roomboter	Dairy fresh butter
Slasaus	Salad dressing
Studentenhaver	Nuts and raisins
Saus	Sauce
Suiker	Sugar
Zout	Salt

Some Cooking Terms

Gebakken	Fried
Gegratineerd	Au gratin
Gehakt	Chopped
Gekookt	Boiled
Geroosterd	Broiled

EATING OUT
Cakes and bread

Appelbol – A whole apple baked in crisp, sweet pastry, then glazed
Appel Enveloppe – A featherlight apple turnover of puff pastry with an apple and raisin filling, generously dusted with icing sugar.
Brood – Bread, of which there is an enormous and appetising variety, including crusty white farmhouse loaves, wholesome wholemeal 'boerenbruin', light French 'stokbrood', some hearty fruit, nut and muesli breads and wickedly sticky banana and apricot loaves.
Chipolata Taart – This is not sausage pie, but a delicious chilled mousse flan
Gember Gebak – Ginger cake
Gevulde Koeken – A small tart of rich almond shortcake, topped with crunchy toasted almonds.
Kerst staaf – A Christmas special: a log shaped cake of light puff pastry, sprinkled with spiced nuts and icing sugar and filled with almond marzipan
Kersentaart – Cherry tart
Kwark Taart – Cheese cake
Mocca Gebak – Mocha cake
Ontbijt koek – A wholesome breakfast cake containing nuts, currants or muesli
Kerst Stolletje – A small yeasted fruit bun sprinkled with icing sugar, which is another Christmas speciality
Roggebrood – Pumpernickel, a moist, rich wholegrain rye bread also available with dried fruit and hazelnuts
Saucijzebroodje – Sausage roll
Slagroom Gebak – A pastry shell with a fruit and whipped cream filling
Vruchten Gebak – Fresh fruit flan

Chapter Eleven
Nightlife

11.1 See Amsterdam lit up

As night falls in Amsterdam, there's no need to curl up with a good book or watch BBC 1 and 2 on cable TV. Low-brow, middle or high, there's an enormous range of night-time action that keeps bubbling till long past midnight.

For a different view of Amsterdam, try a night-time canal cruise to see buildings, monuments and bridges beautifully illuminated. There are several variations on this theme: a one-hour circuit with guided commentary; two hours of Amsterdam by candlelight, with soft music, wine and Dutch cheese; or an expensive 'dinner cruise' nightly during summer till October, or Tuesdays and Fridays during winter.

Show-time

Amsterdam's most startling phenomenon is the wide open Red Light district, a few minutes' walk from Dam Square. If you go there sightseeing, it's advisable to stay on the main canals of Oude Zijde Voorburgwal and Oude Zijde Achterburgwal, and avoid the narrow side alleys. Tourist photography is not appreciated by the local ladies.

There are scores of low-life bars, girls winking at passers-by from every window, and a resident Salvation Army band to supply background music. Policemen have nothing more exciting to do than watch benevolently over the window-shoppers.

Amsterdam has a reputation for tolerance of alternative lifestyles. The attitude is live-and-let-live;

NIGHTLIFE

do your own thing. Cannabis is freely smoked in 'Smoking' coffeeshops, but hard drugs are totally illegal. If you wander by mistake into one of these coffeeshops, beware of their chocolate cakes nicknamed 'pot brownies', which include a twitch of marijuana in the recipe. Some people claim that hash brownies don't do anything but add fibre to your diet, but an innocent consumer could get unexpectedly high.

Amsterdam has few big-time Shows in the Parisian style, but abounds in smaller spots with dancing and cabaret. During a short stay in Amsterdam, simplest policy is to migrate either to Leidseplein, Rembrandtsplein or Thorbeckeplein. Much of the nightlife action is focussed on these squares, and in the streets around. Almost every building beckons with a bar, restaurant, nightclub or cabaret. Happy Hour reigns from 5 to 6 p.m., with offers of two drinks for the price of one.

Reguliersdwarsstraat – running parallel to the Singel flower market from Rembrandsplein to Koenigsplein – is a lively venue, with some of Amsterdam's best gourmet restaurants, and also a number of gay and non-gay bars. For restaurant suggestions, see the previous chapter.

Among the night-spots, entrance fees are mostly quite reasonable, like £3 – so you can easily swing from one to another, taking a drink at each. Every day, Amsterdam offers an average choice of forty performances in the city's selection of theatres, concert halls and jazz clubs. Check the publication 'Amsterdam This Week' for What's On. Films are shown in the original language.

Close to Leidseplein is the Melkweg (the Milky Way), a massive entertainment complex of cinema, disco, art centre, theatre (mostly English-language) and live music.

Started by the hippies in the 60's, it became a centre of the Dutch music industry and still keeps a 'Fringe' image in the arts.

In top price-range is the Lido show, Amsterdam's closest approach to a Parisian dinner-cabaret. Singing waiters double as entertainers between courses, and also perform in the main 70-minute show.

NIGHTLIFE

A lower-cost second show is given on Saturdays at 11.30 p.m., to include a drink but no dinner.

The Lido is part of a newly-built complex in a superb waterfront position close to Leidseplein. The Restaurant Gauguin offers French and Asiatic cuisines.

The Holland Casino includes a traditional gaming room, and also Jackpot slot machines and Bingo. Passport is needed for admittance, minimum age 18, suitable dress.

11.2 The music scene

Amsterdam takes civic pride in its total of 50 theatres, concert halls and jazz clubs that give 15,000 performances and concerts every year.

If you want top-flight opera and ballet, make a special effort to visit the 1600-seat Music Theatre on Waterlooplein, adjoining the Town Hall and overlooking the Amstel River. The Dutch National Ballet is considered one of the best and most versatile companies in Western Europe. Performances by the Netherlands Opera and the Netherlands Dance Theatre are also given here. Other major international companies help fill the annual programme.

Remember also that Amsterdam is home town of two symphony orchestras – the world-famed Royal Concertgebouw Orchestra, founded 1888; and the Netherlands Philharmonic. Both give performances in the Concertgebouw's newly restored building on Van Baerlestraat (opposite Museum Square). The season runs mainly between mid-September and March. However, in recent years a series of performances has been staged in July and August, immediately after the annual Holland Festival of June 1-30. It gives summer visitors a chance to experience the superb acoustics of the Concertgebouw's Great Hall (Grote Zaal).

The Recital Hall of the Concertgebouw, and beautiful city-centre churches, also provide ideal settings for chamber music and organ recitals. Amsterdam has over 40 historic church organs, of which those in the Oude Kerk and the Nieuwe Kerk are especially renowned.

NIGHTLIFE

Interest in contemporary music has increased greatly in recent years, and performers and audiences have found a home in the IJsbreker (located at Weesperzijde 23 – trams 3, 6, 7, 10). The BIM-Huis at Oude Schans 73-77 specialises in improvised jazz music. Other venues such as De Kroeg, Bourbon Street Jazz & Blues Club, Alto and Joseph Lam offer more traditional jazz.

Amsterdam is famed for two other kinds of music; the carillons from ancient towers, and the street music of colourful barrel organs.

11.3 Quenching your thirst

Tourism is thirsty work, and Amsterdam has a huge range of bars and coffeeshops to cater for locals and visitors. Dutch bars are quite different from British pubs. They range from modern designer bars with waiter service, to places which specialise in jazz or blues or background piano, where the music is as important as the drink.

Try sampling the local brew - approximately 3 guilders for a beer - in a traditional 'brown bar' (*bruin kroeg*). There's no mistaking them, with their dark wood-panelled walls, obscurely lit alcoves for those who want to be alone, and even wall to wall sawdust under your feet.

Some bars operate also as cafés where you can get tea or coffee or hot chocolate, and snacks or cakes. Others have gone up-market, and cater for the Dutch yuppie trade. A number of gay bars are clustered in the areas of Rembrandtsplein/Amstel and Kerkstraat.

Most bars serve a selection of Dutch and maybe other lagers; also Dutch spirits (such as the full Bols range), including of course jenever, or Dutch gin, which you drink neat.

It comes in two main sorts - oude jenever (old gin) and jonge jenever (young gin). The young gin is sweeter, because more of the sugar has been left unfermented.

Beware of oude jenever until you're used to it - though even the 'young' version can be pretty potent. Try Bessen (blackcurrant) or Citroen (lemon).

NIGHTLIFE

Specialising in these spirits are *proeflokalen* (tasting houses), originally run by private distilleries, and which normally close around 8 p.m. Be prepared to follow the old custom of leaning over the bar, hands behind your back, to take the first sip from the *borreltje* (small drinking glass).

Below are listed some recommended bars - by no means complete, but then why not make your own discoveries? Most are open until 1 or 2 a.m.

Bars and Cafés

De Tap, Prinsengracht 476
De Blinker, 7 St Barberenstraat
Hans en Greitje, Spiegelgracht 27
De Schutter, Voetboogstraat 13-15
L & B Limited, Korte Leidsedwarsstraat 82

Bars with Music

Joseph Lam Jazz Club, Van Diemenstraat 242
  Dixieland (Fri, Sat only)
Piano Bar Le Maxim, Leidsekruisstraat
  Piano (Closed Sunday)
Café Nol, Westerstraat 109
  Song & Dance/Dutch
Bamboo Bar, 66 Lange Leidsedwarsstraat
  Jazz/Blues
Alto Jazz Café, 115 Korte Leidsedwarsstraat

Brown Bars

Het Molenpad, 653 Prinsengracht
Gollem, Raarnsteeg 4
  Popular due to huge variety of beer available.
de Pilsener Club, Begijnensteeg 4
  Very old decorated in brown with sand on the floor.
de Eland, Prinsengracht 296
  Said to be over 200 years old. Note the worn steps outside, now turned upside down.
Hoppe, Spui 18-20
  Bar and saloon. Gets very busy, so often only standing room.

NIGHTLIFE

Smart Bars
Tend to be rather cosmopolitan, very popular and usually busy.

De Jaren, 20 Nieuwe Doelenstraat
The Lido and Brasseric, by the Leidseplein
L'Opera, Rembrandtsplein 27
Rum Runners, Prinsengracht 277
Harry's American Bar, Spuistraat 285
Luxembourg, Spui 24
Hard Rock Café, Korte Leidsedwarsstraat 28

Nightclubs

Mazzos, 114 Rozengracht
   Small disco with alternative new wave music.
Cash, Leidseplein
   A rather trendy disco situated on the Leidseplein. Smart dress.
Escape, Rembrandtsplein
   Large new disco, jazz-funk and popular music. Live bands occasionally. Great light show. Smart dress.
Odeon, Singel 460
   A large casual disco in a former theatre. Popular music.
IT on Amstelstraat
   A famous gay disco with theme nights for dressing up.

Chapter Twelve
Travel tips

12.1 Clued-up for Amsterdam

Costs
Mostly you'll find Amsterdam a bit more expensive than UK, mainly due to Britain's devaluation of October 1992. But the difference is not big enough to be a deterrent to large numbers of UK visitors. In general, average income-levels are somewhat higher in Holland, and the VAT rate is 20%.

Entrances to the major museum-galleries cost almost £4 each; but younger and elderly age groups can halve the price. If necessary, have passport ready to show you are of student age, or over-65.

Amsterdam city transport – trams and buses – are quite cheap with strip-tickets (see chapter 3), especially as you'll be spending your time almost entirely in the Central Zone. It's worth taking a few minutes to learn the system. Play it right, and you can travel anywhere within the Centrum for the equivalent of about £1.50, including any changes.

If you're on a tightish budget, you can eat at reasonable cost at fast-food outlets of the international chains; otherwise pick some of the restaurant listings suggested in Chapter 10.

What to pack
The weather is very similar to Britain's, but a few degrees cooler. During winter, spring and autumn, be prepared with warm clothing. Even in summer, have a sweater in reserve. Forget about high heels, with all those cobbles. Comfortable, flat footwear is much better.

TRAVEL TIPS

Power points

If you want to use any electric gadgets, pack a plug adaptor. Amsterdam is on 220 volts, but mainly uses the Continental-type 2-pin plug.

Don't worry if your cosmetic, pharmaceutical or film supplies run out. All the major brands are readily available in Amsterdam. A chemist's shop is *Apotheek*.

But take plenty of camera film – UK prices are much cheaper.

If mosquitoes normally have you for summer, bring some repellent. Amsterdam has water everywhere, and insects flourish especially in July and August.

Public lavatories

Mostly impeccable, at museums, restaurants and bars: labelled Dames or Heren or the usual obvious international symbols to help you guess which door is which. An attendant or a wistful saucer will expect to receive a small contribution, like 50 cents, or Dfl 1.00 at weekends.

Local time

Simple enough in summer and winter, Amsterdam is one hour ahead of UK. But Britain does not synchronise with Western Europe on the changeover dates to and from summer time.

So be extra cautious about time differences and airline schedules in March and in a late-September/October period – especially if you hit the weekend when either Europe or Britain is changing the clocks.

Safety and Security

Just like any big city, Amsterdam has a villain quota; but there's no need to go overboard with suspicion of all strangers. However, it's sensible not to make things easy for pickpockets.

Leave any bulk supplies of money in your hotel safe-deposit.

Beware especially on crowded trams and in street markets. In cafés or restaurants, don't hang bags on the backs of chairs.

TRAVEL TIPS

Daily Hours
Most shops open weekdays at 9 a.m., but take the morning off on Monday. Museums vary, so check timings in Chapter 6 or in 'Amsterdam This Week'. Nothing's open on New Year's Day. On other public holidays, most museums open like on Sunday.

Evening mealtimes start around 6 p.m., and restaurants often are taking last orders by 10 p.m. Bars are open till past 1 a.m., discos much later. Trams stop running at midnight.

Tipping
A tip is customary for taxi and motor-coach drivers. In restaurants and cafés, 15% service is automatically included in the price, but it's usual to leave a tip.

12.2 Taking the children

Amsterdam is great for grown-ups. But what's in it for the children? In fact, there's lots that will grab their enthusiasm. How many British kids have ridden on trams, or on canal-boats?

Children enjoy the boat trips, and climbing up church towers, or going to Amsterdam's excellent Zoo called Artis, which includes a 'children's farm' and a superb aquarium with over 2000 different varieties of fish.

Among the choice of museums, consider the Maritime Museum – fascinating for children of all ages – and the Piggybank Museum in Raadhuisstraat behind the Royal Palace. The Rijksmuseum is a big yawn for most youngsters, but is redeemed by the collection of 17th-century dolls' houses on the ground floor.

For entertainment, ask the VVV if any puppet shows or similar productions are performing for younger age-groups.

At summer weekends, there's always plenty for the children in Vondel Park.

For a day trip, consider The Hague, which sounds stuffy but is worth visiting for a stroll round the centre, followed by a tram-ride to Madurodam.

TRAVEL TIPS

Holland's biggest miniature town

Madurodam is a model town that offers a two-mile stroll through a child's paradise in 1/25th scale: docks with ships and boats moving up and down; a tanker ablaze, with a fire-fighting vessel alongside, pouring water on the flames.

For adults, too, Madurodam is fascinating, showing how a typical Dutch town has developed over the centuries: city walls, churches, castles and medieval squares, with polder land and farms on the outskirts. A day can end on Scheveningen beach.

Nearer to Amsterdam, the Volendam excursion is Best Buy, crammed with sights lifted straight from a child's picture-book: gingerbread houses, windmills, people in costume-doll clothing.

12.3 Recommended reading

The following books are suggested for background reading:

The Embarrassment of Riches by Simon Schama (Collins) – a superb and detailed account of Amsterdam's Golden Age: a scholarly but very readable heavyweight volume (3 lbs 4 oz).

The Diary of Anne Frank – the moving story of undercover Jewish family life during the Nazi occupation.

Lust for Life by Irving Stone – a best-selling novelist's version of the van Gogh story.

12.4 Learn some Dutch

Really, there's not the slightest need to learn any Dutch, as it's hard to find anyone who doesn't have at least basic English. But some elementary Dutch is very easy to pick up – particularly if you already know German! Dutch is rather like a stepping-stone between German and English.

The Dutch glue words together, like in German, so that street-names for instance can look terrifying: but they're really quite simple when you break the monster words down into their component parts. Grammar is simpler, closer to English.

TRAVEL TIPS

Basic Dutch

Listed below are some simple words and phrases for those who like going local.

Yes / No	Ja / Nee
Good morning	Goede morgen
Good afternoon	Goede middag
Goodbye	Tot ziens!
How are you?	Hoe gaat het met uw?
Please	Alstublieft
Thank you	Dank u wel / Bedankt
How much	Hoeveel kost?
I am hungry / thirsty	Ik heb honger / dorst
Breakfast	Ontbijt
Dinner	Diner
Sandwich	Broodje
Cup of coffee / tea	Kopje koffie / thee
Dish of the day	Dagschotel
May I have the bill	Mag ik de afrekenen alstublieft
A ticket to...	Een kaartje naar...
One-way ticket	Enkele reis
Return	Retour
Which is the platform for The Hague?	Van welke spoor vertrekk de trein naar Den Haag?
Where's the post office?	Waar is het postkantoor?
Ticket office	Loket
Postcard	Briefkaart
Letter box	Brievenbus
Telephone booth	Telefooncel
Push / Pull	Duwen / Trekken
Hot / Cold	Warm / Koud
Entrance / Exit	Ingang / Uitgang
Emergency exit	Nooduitgang
Left / Right	Links / rechts
No smoking	Niet roken
Exchange office	Wisselkantoor
I come from England	Ik kom uit Engeland

Chapter Thirteen
Sunday in Amsterdam

13.1 The joy of peaceful traffic

If you don't like the sound of traffic, Amsterdam on a Sunday morning is idyllic. Shops are closed, and central Amsterdam is relatively empty even of pedestrians. Morning is great for a really peaceful stroll along the canals. If you have the energy and the inclination, it's an ideal time to rent a bike. Photographers can wander into the road for those perfect pictures, without being mown down.

Sunday afternoons, Amsterdam begins to wake up. Most museums and public galleries open from one p.m. But, beforehand, do check from earlier chapters which museums are open. Normally they are crowded with Amsterdammers, using their Museum Card to keep themselves in tune with culture.

Depending on the season, there are afternoon performances of classical music, opera or ballet. A favourite summertime venue is Vondel Park, best on Sunday when there is always plenty doing, with free entertainment.

From 10 a.m. a Sunday-only Art Market in Spui (trams 1, 2 or 5) operates till 6 p.m. from April till November inclusive. Another Art Market likewise functions in Thorbeckeplein, April till October. That's a colourful corner of Amsterdam, with every building occupied by a café, tavern or restaurant.

Later in the day, all of Amsterdam's nightlife bars and discos are fully operational for Sunday customers. As a last resort, there are always the cinemas, showing the latest releases in their original language.

SUNDAY

13.2 Sunday excursions

On a short break, many visitors prefer to avoid a 'dead' Sunday morning in Amsterdam, and fill the time with an out-of-town excursion. Except for traffic-clogged bulbfields in springtime, and the beach resort of Zandvoort in summer, most other Dutch towns spend Sunday in deep slumber. But it's an excellent time for a tour to Volendam and Marken which are lively on a Sunday morning, with shops open.

Local tour operators also feature a special Sunday morning tour, southeasterly from Amsterdam, through lovely Dutch landscape and affluent dormitory villages. En route past polders where cattle graze below sea level, you pass through 'the garden of Amsterdam' where wealthy merchants in 17th and 18th centuries built country houses on the banks of River Vecht or the lakes of Loosdrecht.

Along a road near Hilversum is the stately mansion of Admiral Tromp, who fought several naval battles against England. Hilversum itself is a very leafy residential town, where famous radio and TV companies are located along an avenue of opulent thatched houses with large gardens.

A similar route by bicycle could include Abcoude, Loenen, Breukelen (home town of the Dutch settlers who founded New York's Brooklyn in 1636), around the Loosdrechtse Lakes to Hilversum, and thence back to Amsterdam via Laren, Blaricum, Naarden and Muiden.

Church Services
Catholic: St John & St Ursula, 30 Begijnhof.
Tel: 6221918. English service 12.15 hrs Sun.

Protestant: English Reformed/Presbyterian Church of Scotland, 48 Begijnhof.
Tel: 6249665. English service 10.30 hrs Sun.

The Anglican Church/Church of England/Christ Church Episcopal, 42 Groenburgwal. Tel: 6248877. English services 10.30 & 19.30 hrs Sun.

Chapter Fourteen
At your service

14.1 Money and banking

There are 100 cents in each guilder.

COINS	**NOTES**
5 cents – *stuivers*	10 guilders
10 cents – *dubbeltjes*	25 guilders
25 cents – *kwaartjes*	50 guilders
1 guilder – *gulden*	100 guilders
2½ guilders – *rijksdaalders*	250 guilders
5 guilders	1000 guilders

The symbol used in shops when marking prices is Fl, short for florin. Thus, 20 Fl is 20 guilders. Dfl or hfl is short for Dutch florin or Dutch guilder.

Changing money
You can change money and travellers cheques at banks, exchange bureaux and larger hotels. You may be asked to show your passport. Commission rates vary greatly, and can be high in hotels, and even higher elsewhere.

Take a minute to learn the economics of changing money.

Banks and bureaux earn their living from a 'spread' between buying and selling rates. The difference between those rates is normally 7%, up to 9%. In addition, banks deduct a flat sum as commission or service charge – usually 3 guilders – making it uneconomic to change small sums of money. You get the full official rates at all branches of leading banks such as Rabobank, AMRO and

INFORMATION

N.M.B. Likewise an honest deal is given by major Post Offices, where a blue sign says Postbank. They likewise pay the normal bank rate less 3 guilders.

Warning: be extremely cautious about dealing with streetside exchange bureaux. Many are tricky operators. Typically they display a notice saying in very large letters NO COMMISSION. Then, in much smaller letters, 'for selling foreign currency'. On the bill-board they prominently display selling rates for dollars, pounds etc.

Trustfully, visitors hand over their dollars or pounds, and then get a double shock when the payslip and guilders are passed through the window. Firstly the rate is the much lower 'buying rate' – usually 9% less than the selling rate. And there'll be a deduction for commission or service charge of something like 9.8%.

Protest is useless. Dealers totally refuse to un-do the transaction. They point to another notice which says, in small-print English or Dutch, that commission is payable on *buying* currencies. It's perfectly legal, but very close to cheating. Don't get caught!

Best currency deals

Outside the regular banking system, the best deals are offered by any of the following:

GWK (Border Exchange Offices – a national financial body) at Schiphol Airport or Central Station – bank rate less 2%.

Branches of Thomas Cook – bank rate less 2%.

Marks & Spencer's on Kalverstraat – bank rate, and definitely no commission.

Pott Change on Rembrandtplein and at 95 Damrak – bank rate, and no charges on buying or selling.

Travellers Cheques

These are a safe way of carrying money, but may be difficult to change late at night or over the weekend. A valid passport is required for exchanging travellers cheques. It is best to take some Dutch guilders to tide you over your first few hours in Amsterdam.

INFORMATION

Credit Cards
Cash can be obtained on presentation of most major credit cards and a valid passport at the GWK Bank in Central Station.

Eurocheques
Eurocheques are the most common method of payment in Holland. They can be obtained from your bank if ordered a few weeks in advance and can be used widely in shops, restaurants etc. when presented with a Eurocheque card.

14.2 Post Office and Telephone

Opening hours: Local post offices are normally open Mon-Fri 9-17 hrs.

General Post Office (near Dam Square)
Singel 250. Tel: 556 33 11
Opening hours: Mon-Fri 8-18 hrs
　　　　　　　　　　Thu 08.30-20.00 hrs
　　　　　　　　　　Sat 9-12 hrs

Long distance calls and telegrams: 24-hours service is available via the rear entrance on Spuistraat. Tram 1, 2, 5, 13 and 17.

Calls to UK from coin boxes
1. Lift receiver.
2. Insert at least 1 Dfl, which gives you approximately one minute. (Dfl 0.25 and 2.50 coins are also accepted.)
3. Dial 00 and wait for the tone to change.
4. Dial 44 (the international code for the UK), plus the appropriate area dialling code minus the first zero; then the local number.
5. A red light indicates that you need to insert more coins to continue your call.

NB. There are no cheap off-peak rates.

Phone cards can be bought for 5, 10 or 25 Guilders, for use in blue phone kiosks.

Calls within Amsterdam: insert Dfl 0.50 and dial the number.

INFORMATION

Emergency Phone Numbers

Police	**0611**
Fire Brigade	**0611**
Ambulance	**0611**
Doctor and Dentist Service	664 21 11
Dentist	664 14 06

Consulates

Great Britain: Koningslaan 44, Tel. 676 43 43

USA: Museumplein 19, Tel. 664 56 61

Useful Telephone Numbers/Information

Taxi – Tel. 677 77 77
Watertaxi – Tel. 622 21 81

Police Headquarters
117 Elandsgracht. Tram 7, 10, 17
Tel. 559 91 11.

Other Police Stations
Central Station area, Warmoesstraat 44-50
Leidseplein area, Lijnbaansgracht 219

Should you have anything stolen you must report it to the Police, for insurance reclaim purposes. A formal declaration will then be issued, to support your claim for compensation.

Lost Property
Waterlooplein 11. Tram 9, Tel. 559 91 11
Open 11-15.30 hrs Mon-Fri.
Open for telephone 12-15.30 hrs.

Losses on Public Transport
Prins Hendrikkade 108-114. Tel. 551 49 11
Open 08.30-16.30 hrs Mon-Fri.

Losses on Trains
Central Station Lost Property, Stationplein 1
Tel. 557 85 44.
Open daily 07.00 to 22.00 hrs.

INFORMATION

14.3 Medical contacts

Should you need to see a doctor, you will have to pay for the consultation. Obtain a receipt both from the doctor and the chemist in order to claim under the terms of any insurance you may have. If you are on a Thomson Citybreak and sizeable funds are required to cover medical expenses, contact the Thomson representative for advice and assistance.

Pharmaceutical Chemists
Late duty chemists operate on a rotating basis. For information on those open contact the 24 hour doctor and dentist service – Tel: 664 21 11.

24 hrs Tourist Medical Service
Sarphatistraat 94. Tel: 612 37 66

Hospitals with First Aid Departments
AMC, Meibergdreef 9. Tel: 566 91 11
V U Ziekenhuis, 1117 Boelelaan. Tel: 548 91 11
Onze Lieve Vrouwe Gasthuis,
179 le Oosterparkstraat. Tel: 599 91 11
Dentists Practice AOC, 167 W.G. Plein
Tel: 616 12 34. Open 06.00-02.00 hrs.

14.4 More information

Contact the local offices of Netherlands Board of Tourism for brochures and specific advice:
Britain – P.O. Box 523, London SW1E 6NT. An information line number 0891-71 7777 costs 39p per minute at cheap rate, otherwise 49p per minute.

U.S.A. East Coast – 355 Lexington Avenue (21st Floor), New York NY 10017. Tel: (212) 370-7367.
U.S.A. Midwest – 225 N Michigan Avenue, Suite 326, Chicago Ill. 60601. Tel: (312) 819-1636.
U.S.A. Westcoast – 9841 Airport Blvd., Suite 103, Los Angeles, CA 90045. Tel: (310) 348-9339.
Canada – 25 Adelaide Street East, Suite 710, Toronto Ont. M5C 1Y2. Tel: (416) 363-1577.